An OPUS book

Moral Philosophy

Moral Philosophy

Second, enlarged edition

D. D. Raphael

Oxford   New York

OXFORD UNIVERSITY PRESS

Oxford University Press, Walton Street, Oxford OX2 6DP

Oxford New York
Athens Auckland Bangkok Bombay
Calcutta Cape Town Dar es Salaam Delhi
Florence Hong Kong Istanbul Karachi
Kuala Lumpur Madras Madrid Melbourne
Mexico City Nairobi Paris Singapore
Taipei Tokyo Toronto

and associated companies in
Berlin Ibadan

Oxford is a trade mark of Oxford University Press

First issued as an Oxford University Press paperback 1981 and simultaneously in
a hardback edition
Paperback reprinted 1982, 1984, 1985, 1987, 1989, 1990
Second, enlarged edition published as an Oxford University Press paperback 1994

British Library Cataloguing in Publication Data
Data available

Library of Congress Cataloging in Publication Data
Raphael, D. D. (David Daiches), 1916–
Moral philosophy / D. D. Raphael.—2nd, enl. ed.
p. cm.—"An OPUS book."
Includes bibliographical references and index.
1. Ethics—Popular works. I. Title.
170—dc20 BJ1025.R36 1994 93–3919
ISBN 0-19-289246-0

10 9 8 7 6 5 4 3

Printed in Great Britain by
Biddles Ltd.
Guildford and King's Lynn

Preface

This book is intended as an introduction to the subject and requires no previous knowledge of philosophy. While I hope that parts of it may interest more experienced readers also, it has been written with an eye to the needs of the beginner. There is no dearth of short books on ethics which are introductory in the sense of paving the way to more advanced works. But there is a dearth of such books which really are suitable for beginners. After trying out various modern textbooks in elementary courses over a long period of years, I have not found any which serves the purpose satisfactorily, and inquiry among colleagues shows that others share my view. So I have drawn upon my teaching experience to try to fill the gap.

London, 1980   D.D.R.

The second edition contains two new chapters, 11 and 12, and a few minor amendments of the text elsewhere.

London, 1993

Contents

Introduction

1 What is moral philosophy ?

Philosophy is a peculiar activity, and one of its peculiarities is that it cannot be easily or simply defined. It has in fact meant rather different things to different people at different times and places. I shall begin by suggesting a view of moral philosophy which I have found helpful, but I must emphasize that my account is not a universally accepted definition. A fair number of present-day philosophers might agree that it is a reasonable way of describing the subject although not necessarily put in the words which they themselves would use. However, this absence of firm agreement on definition does not matter much. The best way to understand the nature of philosophy is to have some experience of doing it.

In my view, the main purpose of philosophy, as practised in the Western tradition, is the critical evaluation of assumptions and arguments. Every society and every cultural group tends to accept without question a number of beliefs. These are taken for granted, instilled in the young as part of their education, and presupposed in the process of forming further ideas. For example, a primitive tribe may assume without question that disastrous events like storms and plagues are caused by angry gods who need to be placated, or (a less common type of belief) that the death of an individual is due to witchcraft practised by another individual. A medieval society in Western Europe would have taken for granted the literal truth of most of the events narrated in the Old and New Testaments. In modern societies most people accept without question that 'seeing is believing', that perception by the senses is the most reliable kind of evidence there is. Philosophy asks us to examine such assumptions, to consider whether we have good reason to follow them. If we find that we have, then we may continue to hold the beliefs, but now with rational assurance instead of unthinking acceptance. If we find that we do not have good reasons, then we should either suspend judgement or seek a new framework of belief.

The questioning of traditional assumptions by philosophers does not just arise out of the blue at any time. It is often due to a conflict between old and new beliefs. In the world of ancient Greece certain itinerant

...ers (called 'sophists', but the word did not initially carry any ...gestion of dishonest argument) found that different societies had ...fferent customs and different systems of law; they were thereby led to query the natural assumption that the rules of one's own society are sacrosanct, of divine origin and absolutely valid. In modern Europe some striking advances of natural science (the Copernican account of the solar system or Darwin's theory of evolution by natural selection) have, at first sight anyway, conflicted with traditional religious beliefs and have led to philosophical questioning. More recently advances in psychology have suggested that some lawbreakers, kleptomaniacs for instance, cannot help it and should not be blamed or punished. Here there is a conflict between (what is claimed to be) new knowledge and traditional assumption in the administration of law.

These conflicts lead us to question beliefs that were traditionally taken for granted. Is theological teaching true? Why should we believe it? Is the new science true? Why should we trust that rather than the old belief? What is reliable evidence? Is there a real conflict here? If so, how do we resolve it?

The resolution of such a conflict may take any of three forms. First, one may decide to retain the old belief and reject the new. Secondly, one may adopt the converse procedure, retaining the new belief and rejecting the old. Or thirdly, one may conclude that there is some truth in each of the two conflicting sets of beliefs but that one or both must be modified so as to iron out the inconsistency between them. Of these three possibilities, the second and the third are the more important in the history of philosophy, and it is easy to see why.

There are, of course, some new beliefs which do not have much of a rational backing, such as the springing up of a new cult among people who are psychologically deprived in one way or another. The fact that such a belief conflicts with traditional ideas will not produce philosophical questioning because there is no suggestion that the new belief rests on better reasons than the old. When a conflict does produce philosophical questioning, it is because the new belief seems to be well grounded. This being so, the first of the three possible reactions – rejecting the new and retaining the old – is not common among philosophers. It is adopted by conservatively-minded persons who have not taken the measure of the rational backing for the new belief. Their attitude cannot win much respect outside their own circle and it tends to dwindle away after a time. People who are moved by rational considerations go for the second or third methods of dealing with the conflict. Either they reject the traditional beliefs, and so produce an inconoclastic or sceptical philosophy; or else they try to reconcile new and old by modification, and so produce a reconstructionist philosophy.

Major movements in philosophy arise in this way from apparent conflict between different beliefs. Philosophy examines critically the assumptions and arguments that have buttressed the opposing beliefs. It asks: 'Why should we believe this? Have we any good reason to do so? Is that a good reason? What is good or sound reasoning?' Critical evaluation may end up negatively, with scepticism – 'We do not have reason to believe this'; or positively, with reconstruction – 'We have good reason, provided that we understand the belief in such a way'.

In either event the conclusion is liable to be criticized. The sceptic, having decided that the traditional belief must go altogether, has to consider critically the suggestion of the reconstructionist that a substantial element of the traditional belief can stand when suitable modifications are made. The reconstructionist in his turn cannot be satisfied with his own solution unless he has shown some serious flaw in the arguments of the sceptic for abandoning the traditional view altogether. A second reconstructionist may agree with the general programme of the first one but may think that it has not been carried out satisfactorily and may propose an alternative. A second sceptic may agree with the broad outlook of the first sceptic but may think that the argument is faulty in some details and needs amendment. For reasons like these, a new movement in philosophy, started off by a conflict between old and new belief, tends to continue of its own accord, generating further critical discussion within the movement itself and more or less divorced from the crisis in thought which was its original impetus. After a time the discussion may become esoteric, scholastic in the bad sense, of interest to the professionals only, and an arid wasteland in the eyes of the layman. Philosophy which has a lasting impact retains a connection with the beliefs of real life.

Reconstructionist philosophy is not always the result of doubt about traditional belief. Jewish and Christian philosophers of the Hellenistic and Middle Ages produced a synthesis of biblical religion and Greek philosophy without having any serious doubts about the former. They were faced with apparent conflicts which they tried to iron out, but most of them were not in the least perturbed about the truth of their traditional religious beliefs. Rather, having seen the rational strength of much Greek philosophy, they concluded that its apparent truth *must* be reconcilable with what they took to be the undoubted truth of revealed religion. This means that the questioning ethos of philosophy is not as thorough as it might be in the religious philosophy of this period. Still, the most important of the medieval religious philosophers do try to give rational grounds for their religious beliefs, as well as to synthesize them with the philosophy of Aristotle.

The critical evaluation characteristic of philosophy begins as a critique of assumptions but then goes on to a critique of argument also. When one asks 'Have we good reasons for accepting this belief?' debate about that is liable to lead to the further question, 'What are good reasons for accepting a belief?' As with beliefs themselves, the criteria for accepting beliefs are often assumed without question, and since there is more than one possible criterion, we need to ask whether all the criteria are equally valid and whether they are valid in the same way. Acceptance of a belief on authority is clearly different from acceptance after proof. It is one thing to accept a belief (e.g. that the universe was created by an omnipotent God) because your Bible, or your supreme priest, says so, and it is quite another thing to accept the same belief, or a similar one, because you have demonstrated it, or have seen and understood a demonstration, by logical reasoning. We might express this difference by distinguishing between 'faith' and 'reason'. But then what about the difference between logical proof and the evidence of observation or experiment? Some propositions can be proved by the exact demonstration employed in mathematics or deductive logic. Others – indeed most of our beliefs – cannot be proved in that way but are supported by the evidence of experience, whether this be common observation or the more specialized observation which a scientist makes when he devises a series of experiments. We should, in the ordinary way of speaking, say that such support by the evidence of experience is a perfectly rational ground for accepting a belief, as is logical proof. But are they 'rational' in the same sense or in the same sort of way? Logical (including mathematical) proof leaves no room for doubt; it produces a necessary result. Empirical evidence (i.e. evidence from 'experience', whether observation or experiment) has a certain 'weight', it leads to a probable conclusion, but leaves room for the possibility of error. Do both methods afford equally good reasons for accepting a belief? Or is one superior to the other, for certain purposes at least; and if so, why? Are we justified in taking both to be superior to acceptance of a belief on authority; and if so, why? These are the sort of questions which constitute the critical evaluation of argument.

The original function of philosophy, as I have described it, is the critical evaluation of assumptions. This leads on to the critique of argument because the question whether there are good reasons for accepting a belief prompts one to ask what is meant (or what should be meant) by a good reason. The latter inquiry is itself one of critical evaluation but is also a quest for the clarification of meaning. That quest plays a large part in philosophy. If you want to know whether there are good reasons for beliefs which have a wide scope – e.g. the belief that the universe was created by God, the belief that every change must have had a cause, the belief that the things which we perceive by the senses are still there when nobody is perceiving them – you need to be clear what you are talking about. To reach a satisfactory answer, you must not only know what is meant by 'good reasons'; you must also know what is meant by the belief which is being scrutinized. Before you can decide whether the belief in God as creator is justified, you must have a reasonably clear notion of what is meant by the terms 'God' and 'creation'. Likewise with the other examples: you need to be clear about the meaning of 'change' and 'cause', of 'perception' and 'things perceived'. You may think that, while the ideas of God and creation are obscure, those of change, cause, and perception are not. But in fact problems do arise for the more mundane ideas also. Take, for example, the idea of the things which we perceive by the senses. When I see a red sunset, are the sun and the clouds themselves red? It is not clear that they are. If they are not, then what are 'the things which I perceive' in such circumstances? The sun and the clouds, or a partly false appearance or representation of sun and clouds? Clarification of this question is obviously very relevant to the original question whether the things which we perceive are still there when nobody is perceiving them.

The clarification of concepts or general ideas is therefore an essential part of philosophy. Philosophers spend a lot of time considering the meaning or the function of words and phrases. Not just any words and phrases. Philosophy is not a science of language as such, like grammar or philology. It attends to those words and phrases which play a key role in the linguistic expression of ideas that call for critical evaluation. Some writings of professional philosophers in recent decades may give the impression of being concerned only with language or meaning; and indeed many of the writers would have said that such linguistic or conceptual analysis is the only task which philosophy can undertake profitably. That view of philosophy is less fashionable nowadays and I certainly do not agree with it myself. However, there is this to be said for it. In its basic aim of critically evaluating beliefs of wide scope, philosophy seems to make no progress; it appears to go round in circles, endlessly debating old problems about mind and matter, knowledge and opinion, truth, causation, free will, values in general and certain values in particular. But in its subsidiary aim of clarifying concepts it does make definite and visible progress. I believe that the impression of going round in circles on the more basic problems is an illusion. There is progress, though it is very gradual and therefore not easily perceived. The debate goes round in a spiral rather than a circle. That is to say, it does change position and make a winding progress. Such change as does take place is almost always due to progress in the clarification of concepts. The long time spent on the meaning of general terms is far from wasted. Age-old debates in philosophy are rarely (I do not say never) settled, but they are clarified. Even though doubts are not resolved, at least one is no longer in a fog.

On this question of progress, philosophy appears to be different from science, and I think the appearance is well founded. Yet there is a very important respect in which philosophy and science are alike. Both of them are essentially rational enterprises. Rationality is the hallmark of the spirit which pervades both philosophy and science. In this respect philosophy differs from religion and imaginative literature (or art generally) as much as science does. I do not mean that religion and art are altogether irrational or non-rational; I mean that they do not always treat rationality as the overriding aim, while philosophy and science do. Nor do I imply that philosophy differs in every way from religion and art as much as science does; that would be a gross distortion. Nevertheless, the common character of philosophy and science in making rationality essential is far more significant than the differences between them. Their rationality lies in two things, the requirement of consistency and the pursuit of truth. Consistency is a matter of internal coherence and is tested by logic. Truth is a matter of conformity to relevant facts and is tested by observation.

In their practice philosophy and science differ in the relative emphasis given to the two aspects of rationality. Philosophy puts more emphasis on the use of logic because philosophers, unlike scientists, are not in a position to concentrate on the observation of a special field of knowledge. Philosophy leaves that to the different sciences and is usually prepared to accept the empirical data of the sciences as material to work upon. This difference of emphasis in practice does not mean that philosophy and empirical science differ in the relative importance attached to consistency and to truth. Both aims are essential for rational inquiry. There is no question of rating one more highly than the other. The difference of emphasis is purely one of practicability. It is, in a way, a division of labour. Not that scientists cannot do logic; mathematicians are doing it all the time, and most empirical sciences draw heavily on the techniques of mathematics. But there are some kinds of logical inquiry that come more easily to philosophers because their subject has a wider scope than any single science.

This question of scope is another respect, then, in which philosophy and science differ. Science does not need philosophy in order to be self-critical or in order to clarify its concepts. But the practitioner of a particular science is not so likely to see, or to be able to cope with, apparent inconsistencies between two general fields of science (e.g. between the physical sciences and the biological in their ideas of giving an explanation), or between his field of science and some other well-established body of thought (e.g. between psychology and law on responsibility for action). The philosopher can take a more overall view and is accustomed to looking for changes in the use of very general concepts such as explanation or responsibility.

But a philosopher cannot rely on logical analysis alone. If his questions and suggestions are to be of any interest to people more expert in a particular field, he must have a reasonable knowledge of what he is talking about. The great philosophers of the past were often expert in some special field: Aristotle in biology, Descartes and Leibniz in mathematics. It is no good thinking about changes in the concept of matter if you do not know something of physics and its history; or about the concept of criminal responsibility if you do not know something of law. Certain concepts, however, concern things of which we all have adequate knowledge in our everyday life: the concept of knowledge itself and the contrasting one of error, the concepts of truth and falsity, of persons and things, of right and wrong.

We are all liable to come up against conflicts of the kind I described earlier, and to wonder whether we are justified in retaining old beliefs which we formerly took for granted but which now appear to be challenged by new ideas. That is to say, we all philosophize at times in a crude way. So it is worth having a taste of the attempt to do so less crudely. It would not do for everyone to play the philosopher all the time. But everyone ought, as Descartes said, to go in for some critical examination of his ideas at least once in his life.

So far I have talked about philosophy in general. The view which I have suggested is that philosophy is first, the critical evaluation of assumptions and argument, and second, but in fact extensively and with more obvious success, the clarification of concepts which have a key role in the notions subjected to critical evaluation.

I want now to distinguish moral philosophy from philosophy in general. When I gave examples of conflict between old and new beliefs, some concerned beliefs about fact, beliefs about what is the case, while others concerned beliefs about values or norms, beliefs about the way we ought to behave. The conflict between the Copernican and the Ptolemaic theories of astronomy, or the conflict between Darwin's theory of evolution by natural selection and the traditional theological doctrine that different species were separately created, concerns matters of fact. The conflict between the sophists' view that justice is conventional, relative to society, and the traditional view that it is absolute, or the conflict between old and new beliefs about kleptomaniacs, whether they should be given punishment or medical treatment, is a conflict about norms. Or rather, the second group of beliefs are mixed; they are beliefs both about fact (what is the case) and about norms (what should be done). The debate about justice is obviously about an idea of value, but it also includes dispute on the factual question whether the acknowledged differences in the legal codes of different societies do or do not imply differences in fundamental moral outlook. The debate about kleptomaniacs involves a difference of view about the way in which society ought to treat a group of lawbreakers, but it is also a dispute on the question whether these lawbreakers are responsible for their actions, whether or not they have the power to refrain from stealing when faced with temptation, and that question is a factual one. Such a mixture of two kinds of subject-matter makes it all the more necessary to analyse and clarify the concepts used.

Moral philosophy is philosophical inquiry about norms or values, about ideas of right and wrong, good and bad, what should and what should not be done. Philosophy in fact has a number of branches, but in my view these can be grouped into two main divisions, the philosophy of knowledge and the philosophy of practice. The philosophy of knowledge is concerned with the critique of assumptions about matters of fact and also with the critique of argument. It includes epistemology (the theory of knowledge), metaphysics (a name used both for an inquiry into very general ideas of reality and for one into the relationships between different branches of knowledge), the philosophy of science, philosophical psychology (or 'philosophy of mind') and philosophical logic (the critique of argument). The philosophy of practice is concerned with the critique of assumptions about norms or values, which are mostly used to guide practice. It includes ethics, social and political philosophy, and the philosophy of law. As we have seen, however, debate about values is apt to involve debate about certain matters of fact also.

The twofold classification of the branches of philosophy into philosophy of knowledge and philosophy of practice is not altogether exhaustive. Aesthetics (the philosophy of beauty and art) does not fit easily into either of the two divisions. Aesthetics seems akin to ethics since both inquire into judgements of value rather than judgements of fact, but the notions which aesthetics examines are at least as much concerned with contemplation as with practice. One could include aesthetics in the second main division of philosophy by replacing the distinction between knowledge and practice by the distinction between fact and value, but that suggestion, too, runs into difficulties. The philosophy of knowledge, as I have called it, has its own ideas of value which come under scrutiny, such as the ideas of truth and of validity or cogency in reasoning. On the other side, debate about moral and legal values or norms also involves debate about questions of fact.

Some people use the term 'moral philosophy' as synonymous with 'ethics', the philosophical discussion of assumptions about right and wrong, good and bad, considered as general ideas and as applied in the private life of individuals. In the history of the subject the term has been used more widely, to cover also the discussion of normative ideas (i.e. ideas of value or of what ought to be done) in organized social life as well as in private relationships; in particular it has included political and legal philosophy. In some continental countries the central academic discipline touching all these subjects is called the philosophy of 'law', but the term here translated as 'law' (French *droit*, German *Recht*) includes the idea of moral principle that enters into law. Anyway, it seems to me that the point of studying moral philosophy is more apparent when one sees the connections between abstract ethics and philosophical problems about law and government. So I shall in this book follow the traditional wider use of the expression 'moral philosophy', showing how the ideas of ethics are connected with some problems of political and legal philosophy.

Is moral philosophy a theoretical or a practical inquiry? It is certainly not practical in any straightforward sense. Moral philosophy cannot, and does not try to, tell us what we ought to do. We must decide that for ourselves. Nevertheless moral philosophy is not purely theoretical. Most people do not study the subject simply for the fun of it. The inquiry arises from a problem of real life. If I have come to doubt moral beliefs which I previously took for granted, and if I therefore ask whether there are good reasons for or against acceptance, I seriously want to know what I should believe about right and wrong. To ask, in the face of conflicting codes of conduct, whether there is good reason to accept one and reject the rest, is virtually to ask which, if any, is really right. If we succeeded in showing that one was really right, that would come pretty close to showing how we ought to behave. So it is not surprising that Plato, for instance, should describe moral philosophy as inquiring 'how we ought to live' (*Republic*, 352 D).

Moral philosophy is not in fact able to give a conclusive answer to that inquiry. In other words, it cannot fully achieve its primary aim of critically evaluating normative assumptions. But even partial achievement can be of practical use. Philosophical debate can reach a firm negative conclusion that one particular set of beliefs should be rejected because it is internally inconsistent or because it rests on a factual assumption which is false. The conclusion is a negative one, showing us only what *not* to accept. It does not show us what positive belief should rationally be held. Yet the negative conclusion is of practical use in narrowing down the range of viable options from which we must still make a choice.

Moral philosophy also makes definite progress in its secondary aim of clarifying concepts, and this often helps individuals to make their own decisions on the more practical questions. We shall see in later chapters that clarification of an idea like justice can be crucial in helping one to decide between two rival theories of ethics as a whole. Indirectly, then, moral philosophy does have some practical effect.

But one should not expect too much from it. Students sometimes come to moral philosophy with the hope that it will solve their practical problems, will show them what to believe and what to do. The hope is forlorn. All philosophical theories are subject to criticism. You cannot absolutely prove any positive conclusion in moral philosophy, or in philosophy generally, any more than you can in empirical science (as distinguished from the formal science of mathematics). What you can do, both in philosophy and in empirical science, is to disprove some suggestions and to show up some confusions. But science can often go much further than philosophy in the process of eliminating hypotheses. In philosophy, far more than in science, one is left in the end with a number of possible theories, none of them proved, none of them definitely disproved. The individual must then decide for himself which, if any, to accept. The choice is much more difficult than in science because there is little hard evidence. When inquirers have seen how to make a topic susceptible to hard evidence and so to find a clear path of progress, the topic ceases to be part of philosophy and becomes the subject of a special science. At least that is what happens with problems about fact. Problems about values or norms for practice do not pass from philosophy to science for reasons which will become apparent in the next chapter. But so far as philosophy is concerned, the end result is similar both in the philosophy of knowledge and in the philosophy of practice. If you are faced with a dilemma on what is the right thing to do, moral philosophy will not find a decision for you. What it can do is to remove some confusions and clarify some obscurities, so that the options stand out more plainly. But then the actual choice between them is something you must make yourself.

So do not expect moral philosophy to solve the practical problems of life or to be a crutch on which you can lean. A study of philosophy makes it more necessary, not less, to stand on your own feet, to be self-critical, and to be obliged to choose for yourself. It makes you more rational, more responsible, more of a human being.

Values and facts

2 Naturalism and rationalism

Philosophy adopts a critical attitude towards beliefs which have previously been taken for granted. Moral philosophy does this with beliefs about right and wrong, good and bad, what is to be done and what is not to be done. The critical questioning of assumptions tends to arise when there is an apparent conflict between an old idea and a new one. Here are a couple of examples. In ancient Greek society, as in many others, it was generally taken for granted that moral rules were absolute and reflected the order of the universe as a whole. When those itinerant teachers called sophists travelled about, in different Greek cities and in non-Greek lands, they found that moral codes and systems of law differed in different societies. This led them to question the old belief that moral rules are absolute and universal. The same sort of thing can happen in modern Western society. One is liable to take it for granted that fundamental moral principles, such as the prohibition against killing people, are absolute and are universally recognized as such. Of course, we all know that primitive tribes, and even civilized nations at war, think that the absolute prohibition applies only within one's own group, but at least to that limited extent, we suppose, the principle is universally accepted as self-evident. So it comes as a surprise to learn from social anthropology that some tribes have approved of killing the old members of their society, or to learn from ancient history that the Spartans exposed weakly infants to die on the mountainside.

One may thus come to doubt the old assumption that basic moral principles are absolute – objectively valid for all time and all peoples. But how do you test the belief? How do you set about finding good reasons for acceptance or rejection? We know how to test doubtful beliefs about matters of fact. If, for instance, you doubt a traveller's tale that the Pygmies of the Congo River Basin are never taller than five feet, you can test it by going and seeing for yourself. (You will find that the tale is an exaggeration.) You cannot do this with values. You cannot see with your eyes whether killing people is right or wrong.

Of course, there are relevant things which you can see with your eyes. If differences of moral belief and practice are reported, you can go and look in order to check the accuracy of the report. You can go and see for yourself whether it is a mere traveller's tale that among the Chukchi people of Siberia the old and the infirm are still put to death (as they certainly used to be) and accept it as a matter of course; that in France every married man has a mistress as well as a wife (this always was just a traveller's tale); or that in an Israeli kibbutz people work without receiving wages. That is to say, you can observe differences of behaviour.

This includes the observation of evidence for moral beliefs. You cannot observe the beliefs themselves but you can observe what people say in expressing their beliefs, and you can observe from the rest of their behaviour whether their statements seem sincere or insincere. For example, you can observe that the Samoans not only practise a different sexual code from ours but also say (if you ask them) that it is right and proper, and display no signs of guilt feeling about it; or that the Israeli kibbutzniks insist on the superior morality of their way of life and that few of them are tempted to work in the towns where they could earn money and have a materially higher standard of living.

We can observe differences of behaviour and the evidence for differences of belief. But if we come to have doubts about the truth of our own moral code, it is not of much help to confirm that some other people have different moral beliefs. Our problem is not to find out what *do* we (or *did* we) believe and what *do* others believe. It is to find out what *should* we believe. Not what we or the Samoans *think* is right, but what we *ought* to think is right, what (if anything) is really right. We want a test for norms or values, not for facts.

People used to think that the earth was flat. We can present good evidence for the view that the earth is really spherical (more or less). What evidence can we present for the view that killing elderly people or weakly infants is really wrong, despite the practices and beliefs of some societies? With the flat-earth example, observation can be corrected by observation. At first sight the earth looks flat; but then we can take account of the difference in the horizon seen from sea level and from a hill top, of watching the hull of a ship disappear over the horizon earlier than the mast, of sailing round the world, of seeing the earth from a lunar space-station. What sort of observation would serve the same purpose for testing moral beliefs? We do not see or touch rightness or wrongness. We do not reach our moral beliefs from the evidence of the senses.

No, but perhaps we reach them from the evidence of a different kind of experience, the experience of feeling or emotion. We have feelings of approval for some actions and states of affairs, feelings of disapproval for others. The same sort of thing applies to aesthetic judgements. When we judge that Beethoven's Fifth Symphony, or a sunset, is beautiful, we do not hear the beauty of the one or see the beauty of the other. We hear the sounds of the symphony and we see the colours of the sunset; but we *feel* aesthetically moved. So perhaps we should say that we *feel* morally moved when we observe an act of kindness or one of cruelty.

This view has an important implication. Feelings are subjective. There are the proverbial expressions: 'beauty is in the eye (meaning the mind, not the physical eye) of the beholder'; 'there is no disputing about tastes'. You like coffee; I like tea. The Spartans approved of exposing weakly infants; we disapprove. So the theory that moral judgements, like aesthetic judgements, depend on the evidence of feeling, has the consequence that they are subjective, relative to the individuals or groups who have the feelings; there is no such thing as an objectively true morality. The status of moral norms is completely different from that of scientific laws and theories. Scientific theories aim at objective truth and have a fair chance of reaching it. Established scientific laws are taken to be objectively true; they may have to be modified in the light of later discovery, but they do depend on objective evidence, not on the subjective feelings of particular individuals or groups.

But is the difference altogether clear? Scientific theories, both in their initial hypotheses and in their final established form as laws, depend upon observation (including observation in experiment). Observation is a matter of perception by the senses. Is not that subjective, too? A colour-blind man cannot distinguish between red and green. Nobody can do so in the dark. But then there are 'standard' perceptions which we take to be objective: what an observer with normal vision sees in a good light.

Does 'normal vision' here simply mean the kind of vision possessed by most observers? Is it a question of numbers? Is the reaction of the majority taken to be 'objective' just because they are a majority? No, this is not what 'normal vision' means. The objectivity attributed to normal vision is not a question of numbers, of giving in to the big battalions. If most people were colour-blind, or myopic, we should not treat their visual perceptions as more trustworthy than the perceptions of the few with a finer discrimination. Take the analogy of hearing. Few people have 'perfect pitch' in discriminating between musical tones, but we trust the hearing of those few more than that of the majority. The objectivity attributed to some kinds of perceptual capacity as contrasted with others, is a matter of recognizing superior ability to discriminate, to make distinctions which arise from real differences in the object of perception.

Even so, sense-perception is still subjective, is it not, in depending on human sense-organs? Grass is seen as green by a person with normal vision, but since that observation depends on the structure of the human eye, are we properly entitled to say that the green colour is objective, is in the grass itself? Perhaps not, but at any rate there is something in the grass which causes a normal human eye to see it as green and not as blue. Even if we say that the qualities made known to us in sense-perception are themselves subjective, nevertheless the discrimination of sense-perception is evidence for objective distinctions in the things perceived.

Is the discrimination of moral approval and disapproval similar to or different from the discrimination of sense-perception? I see somebody pulling a cat's tail and I disapprove. My feeling of disapproval is no doubt subjective, depending on my make-up. So is my visual perception of the cat as ginger-coloured. That visual perception, however, depends not only on something in the physical structure of my eye, but also on something in the physical structure of the cat which causes me to see the ginger colour. Does my feeling of disapproval likewise depend partly on something in the action of pulling the cat's tail which causes me to feel disapproval? Read what David Hume, an eighteenth-century philosopher, has to say:

Take any action allowed to be vicious: wilful murder, for instance. Examine it in all lights, and see if you can find that matter of fact, or real existence, which you call *vice*. In whichever way you take it, you find only certain passions, motives, volitions and thoughts. There is no other matter of fact in the case. The vice entirely escapes you, as long as you consider the object. You never can find it, till you turn your reflection into your own breast, and find a sentiment of disapprobation, which arises in you, towards this action. Here is a matter of fact; but it is the object of feeling, not of reason. It lies in yourself, not in the object. So that when you pronounce any action or character to be vicious, you mean nothing, but that from the constitution of your nature you have a feeling or sentiment of blame from the contemplation of it. Vice and virtue, therefore, may be compared to sounds, colours, heat and cold, which, according to modern philosophy, are not qualities in objects, but perceptions in the mind . . . (*Treatise of Human Nature*, III.i.1).

He writes as if the feeling of disapprobation or blame were entirely due to the natural constitution of the observer and not also dependent upon some fact about the object. But at the same time he writes as if there were a straightforward analogy between moral sentiment and sense-perception, between the supposed quality of vice and the supposed qualities of colours and sounds. He does not take account, here, of the discriminatory character of perception as evidence of *some* difference in the character of the objects perceived. A person of normal vision sees grass as green and tomatoes as red. A person of normal sentiment feels disapproval of murder and approval of saving life. Hume would, of course, agree that the act of murder is objectively different from the act of saving life, and in other parts of his ethical theory he shows how the consequences of actions (happy consequences in the case of saving life, unhappy consequences in the case of murder) engage the sympathy or antipathy of the observer and thereby cause him to feel approval or disapproval. Hume's point, in the passage quoted above, is that none of the immediately present facts (the murderer's feeling of envy, his desire to steal the victim's money, his willed act of firing a gun, his thoughts of what to do with the body) constitute the quality of being vicious which we attribute to the murderer. Hume's analogy with the perceived qualities of sounds, colours, heat and cold, implies that he would say the same of them; but in fact the parallel is not exact. One may say (I think it is correct to say) that the vibrations in the air which cause a listener to hear a particular sound are not the same as the heard sound; that the physical wavelength of light which causes the observer of a tomato, if he has normal vision, to see it as red is not the same as the red colour. Nevertheless there is a strict correlation between the physical cause (or rather, part-cause) and the perceived effect. A listener with normal hearing will hear that particular sound only if his ear is affected by vibrations of that particular character; an observer with normal vision will see that shade of red only if his eye is affected by light of that particular wavelength. There is no strict parallel to this in moral sentiments. We tend to have the feeling of disapproval, and might speak of viciousness, when we observe or hear of a number of different types of action: murder, robbery, deceit, slander, and so on. We might reflect that all these actions are alike in causing unhappy consequences for other persons, and we might think it likely that this common character is what makes us react in the same way. This indirect connection is not strictly analogous to the direct causal effect of the wavelength of light on vision or of vibrations in the air on hearing. Nevertheless it suggests that moral judgement, just as much as sense-perception, can be subjective in one sense and objective in another.

This would hold good if we could properly speak of a normal standard of moral judgement, as we can of vision. But is not moral (like aesthetic) judgement *more* subjective than the judgements of perception? There is much more disagreement in what people judge (or feel) to be right and wrong than there is in their perception of colours. One can say that a sadist is abnormal in his feelings, as a colour-blind person is in his vision; but is it clear that we can say this of the Spartans who exposed weak infants or of the Chukchi who thought it right to kill elderly and infirm kinsmen? When there are so many differences in the moral codes of different societies, how can we regard our own, or any other, as the normal or standard way of thinking?

The differences in moral codes do not in fact go as far as appears superficially. The Spartans placed a high value on the preservation of their society and thought that, since the weak were burdens on society, the survival of the weak would threaten the preservation of their society. (They inhabited a barren land with a precarious economy.) The same may have been true of the Chukchi. It seems that their overt reason for killing the old and the infirm was a belief that there was an afterlife only for those who had met a violent death. But this religious doctrine may well have been an unconscious rationalization of economic pressure. The moral thinking of all societies gives a high value to preservation of the social group as a whole. This is not to say that all societies give it an overriding value so as to be ready to sacrifice individuals for the sake of social survival. Different societies and different groups do differ in the relative weight attached to values that can compete with each other. And, of course, they do not all have to face the same dilemmas; a modern Western society does not live near the margin of subsistence, as the ancient Spartans did, so that the preservation of handicapped children does not have to be set against any real risk of the non-survival of the society as a whole. If we put aside the differences of judgement in the relative weight given to possibly conflicting principles, and if we consider simply the principles themselves which have some value in the moral codes of different societies, the underlying similarities are quite striking. All societies think that it is wrong to hurt members of their own group at least (or to kill them unless there are morally compelling reasons); that it is right to keep faith; that the needy should be helped; that people who deliberately flout the accepted rules should be punished. There are, however, some principles which can be found only in what we should call 'more advanced' systems of ethics and religion: for example, the principle of forgiving one's enemies. The same thing applies to the widening of the scope of moral principles beyond one's own society so as to embrace mankind at large.

The differences between moral codes, then, are not as radical as appears at first sight, and the underlying similarities suggest that perhaps after all there is some near-universality in moral judgement, as there is in sense-perception. The picture is much the same when we look at differences of moral ideas within a single society. In our own society, for example, there is quite a wide diversity of moral judgement, just as there is between one society and another. Here, too, one is inclined at first to note the contrast with perception. When the colour-blind man sees things differently from the rest of us, we can say his vision is abnormal. When the man with perfect pitch hears differences of sound which the rest of us do not, we can easily acknowledge that his sense of hearing is finer or more true. But when egalitarians and élitists differ in their moral judgements, surely neither is entitled to say that the moral outlook of the other group is abnormal or is incapable of discerning nuances which are really there. In fact, however, the difference in their moral outlook is not as stark as appears on the surface. If you attend to their arguments in debate, you will find that each group acknowledges that there is a genuine value on each side of the dispute. They differ mainly in the comparative weight attached to the conflicting values.

So the variations in moral judgement, both between different societies and within a single society, are not quite as thoroughgoing as they look. More to the point, when comparing disagreement in value judgements with disagreement about matters of fact, is the difficulty that it is hard to find an objective test for resolving the disagreement. If a colour-blind man is pig-headed and insists that there is no difference between red and green, he can be shown the differences of wavelength as recorded on an instrument. So too with a tone-deaf person. But what can you do to convince someone who thinks there is nothing wrong in pulling a cat's tail? You can tell him that it causes pain; and if he questions this, you can point to the cat's squeals as evidence of pain. But suppose he says: 'Very well, it causes pain. So what?' How can you show him that if his action causes pain, it is wrong? You may say that he would not like being caused pain. But he might reply: 'No, I would not like it, and fortunately I am not on the other end of that tail.' You may tell him that if he gives pain to others, they will pain him if and when they can. But this is an appeal to prudence, to self-interest, not to morality. The appeal to self-interest is designed to make him alter his behaviour out of fear, not out of moral conviction. How can you lead him to feel moral disapproval rather than fear?

Perhaps you can do so by engaging his sympathy. Hume and others give an account of moral approval and disapproval in terms of general tendencies of human nature. We all (or nearly all) want to be happy, to enjoy pleasure and avoid pain. We all have a natural tendency to sympathize with the similar wishes and feelings of other people (and animals), and this is why we approve of helping people to get what they want and why we disapprove of doing things to them which go against their wishes. According to this view, the feeling of moral approval is a result of the natural tendency to sympathize. Sympathy is a sharing, in imagination, of the feelings of others. We imagine ourselves in their shoes and so come to feel as they feel. If they are pleased we feel pleased; and if their pleasure has been caused by the action of some third person, we warm towards him and his action, we approve of what he has done. If they are pained we feel pained; and if their pain has been caused by the action of some third person, we feel hostile towards him and his action, we disapprove of what he has done.

Such a view of moral judgement is a version of Naturalism. It makes ethics depend on 'human nature', on psychology.[1] An account in terms of sympathy is not the only version of naturalism. There are different conceptions of human nature. One may say, with Hume and his friend Adam Smith, that sympathy is a key factor in human nature, especially as human nature affects social life, and that this factor of sympathy is the most important thing for ethics. Or one may try to say, as a number of philosophers have, that human nature is at root entirely egoistic, that people just want pleasure and power for themselves, and that morality is the result of competition and fear. On this view there is no real difference between morality and prudence. Moral disapproval of hurting others can only be based on calculations of self-interest. If the man who pulls the cat's tail can be made to see that he runs the risk of being scratched by the cat later on, and if he desists from his tail-pulling for that reason, he has reached a moral position. Moral disapproval is a function of self-interested fear.

We shall come back later to the dispute between these two versions of naturalism. For the present it is enough to note what they have in common. They both give an account of ethics in terms of human psychology, of natural feelings and desires. According to them, ethics is wholly dependent on human nature. The variations in moral codes are due to differing social conditions, while the underlying uniformity of these codes is due to the possession, by nearly all human beings, of the same basic psychological tendencies.

As against naturalistic theories of ethics, there are views that ethics contains some absolute truth, that moral values (if not other values) have a foundation in the nature of the universe or in the nature of God, not simply in human nature, which might have been other than it is. Such views have been held by some (not all) theologians and by philosophers called Rationalists.

In the theory of knowledge, a philosophical rationalist holds that genuine knowledge is acquired by reason and is a matter of necessary truth. Examples of such knowledge are the truths of mathematics and of formal logic. In the view of the rationalist, these are truths about the world and they are superior to the information which we receive from sense-perception because their truth is necessary and universal. All the information which is acquired by the senses, or built upon the data of the senses, is not the object of knowledge properly speaking, because it is not necessary and universal. The initial data apply only to individual perceptions, and when we generalize we can only reach conclusions of

[1] In some modern writings about ethics, 'naturalism' is used more narrowly to refer to theories which *define* value terms as equivalent to expressions describing a natural fact, e.g. theories which say that 'good' means the same as 'pleasant' or 'desired'.

probability, which may be falsified. The information gained from the senses is not necessary but 'contingent'; i.e. it happens to be true on a particular occasion or on a number of occasions, but it might not have been true and it could turn out to be false in some instances.

This view of Rationalism, the philosophy of reason, is opposed by that of Empiricism, the philosophy of experience. Empiricists hold that genuine knowledge must depend upon the experience of sense-perception or feeling. Such knowledge is indeed not necessary and universal but it is information about the real world. The truths of pure mathematics and formal logic are necessary and universal because they do not give us information about the world. They depend on definition and artificial rules. They are useful devices, much of which can be applied to the real world but not so as to yield genuinely additional knowledge. The effect of applying mathematics and logic to our information about the world is to reassemble that information in new ways. Genuine additional information must come from further experience.

In the theory of ethics, empiricism appears as naturalism. For the purpose of explaining the concepts of ethics, the kind of experience which is most relevant is not the experience of the senses but that of feeling and desire. Philosophers who are empiricists in the theory of knowledge therefore tend to be naturalists in the theory of ethics.

The rationalist is impressed by the fact that moral judgements often appear to be necessarily true. They differ from the data of perception or facts about human psychology, which are only contingently true. It happens that grass is green, but the colour might have been different; just as it happens that the leaves of most trees are green, but some are red and others grey. It happens that men are benevolent and sympathetic as well as self-seeking, but they might not have been so, as we see from examples of abnormal people who are malicious and sadistic. By contrast, the rationalist argues, it is not a contingent matter that love is good and hate bad, that helping the weak is right and torturing people (or cats) is wrong, that we ought to tell the truth and keep our promises. These things, he says, are necessarily true.

The extent of disagreement in value judgements suggests that they are far from being necessarily true. Why does the rationalist think that they are? The typical rationalist has been impressed by two things. (1) Judgements of value cannot be verified in sense-perception, as can judgements of empirical fact such as 'The grass is green', 'The leaves of the copper-beech are reddish-brown'. And yet we talk, and think, as if we had firm knowledge about them. A man might well say: 'Of course we all know that love is good and hate is bad; how could this not be so?' (2) Moral judgement can often be compared with mathematical judgement, which likewise is not verifiable in sense-perception (because it goes beyond the contingent and particular to the necessary and universal). A mathematical judgement, the rationalist argues, is either reached by deduction or is seen to be self-evident. A simple example of a judgement reached by deduction is this: 'The third side of a triangle must be shorter than the sum of the other two sides because a straight line is the shortest distance between two points.' And a simple example of a self-evident judgement (in the view of the rationalist) would be the premiss of that argument, namely: 'A straight line is the shortest distance between two points.' Similarly, the rationalist goes on, the moral judgement 'You ought to be on time for our meeting because you promised it' is a simple piece of deductive reasoning, and the general premiss on which it depends, 'One ought to keep promises', is a self-evident truth. The conclusion of a deductive inference follows necessarily from its premisses, and a self-evident proposition is one which is necessarily true.

The first step in the rationalist's argument, as presented here, is the fact that value judgements do not depend on experience in the form of sense-perception. But what about the apparently plausible suggestion that they depend instead on the experience of feeling? Moral and aesthetic judgements seem to belong together, and it is common enough to refer to aesthetic judgements as matters of taste. Some matters of taste depend on a simple and fairly immediate reaction, while others are the result of cultivation, but in either event taste has to do with feeling. In a cultivated taste, whether for works of art or for *recherché* food and drink, what is cultivated is a liking, a form of pleasure. Why should we not follow the naturalist in making the validity of value judgements depend on taste and ultimately on feeling?

Although the suggestion looks promising at first sight, it sits uneasily on moral judgements. If someone says it is wrong to pull the cat's tail (or Mary's pigtail), he would not think of this as being like an expression of distaste. Suppose you hear allegations that the police have tortured some suspects in order to extract confessions from them, and you say: 'Torturing suspects is wrong.' It would be inane for the head of the police force to counter with the remark: 'So you feel distaste for it, do you? Well, I do not.' You would want to reply: 'What I *feel* and what you *feel* are irrelevant. I said it is *wrong*.'

We would not be so confident that the suggestion is irrelevant to aesthetic judgements. Suppose two people disagree about the merits of a piece of jazz or pop music. One says that it is beautiful, and the other that it is an appalling noise. The first speaker might then rejoin: 'So you don't like it? Well, I do.' The second speaker would not think that this was an absurd distortion of their disagreement. There are, however, many aesthetic judgements which seem to go beyond the expression of individual liking. If someone describes as beautiful a work of art which would commonly be called great (Michelangelo's Pietà, for instance), he is not referring simply to his own feelings; his judgement includes an expectation that others will share his reaction, or even a sort of claim that they should do so. But at other times the use of the word 'beautiful' carries no such implication. Perhaps this is more obvious with aesthetic judgements of the comic. We do not expect that others necessarily will, still less that they should, share our sense of what is funny. One man's wit is another man's boredom. Puns raise the spirits of some, the hackles of others.

Aesthetic judgements, then, cover a spectrum, one end of which is readily allowed to be subjective. Ethical judgements are different. When we take genuine examples of them, they cannot be treated as expressions of individual taste. Whether justifiably or not, they claim to be valid for everyone on all like occasions. There is a universality in what they intend to say. That is why the rationalist compares them with mathematical judgements, which are likewise universal in meaning. '2 + 2 = 4' means that *any* two things added to any other two will make four things. Universality often (not always, though always in mathematics – for reasons which need not concern us here) goes along with necessity. The mathematical proposition means that the addition of any two and two *must* make four. The rationalist points to a similarity in moral judgements. The judgement that you ought to do an action because you promised (or because it is helping someone in need, etc.) is not a contingent judgement any more than it is confined to the particular case. One is not saying 'It so happens that you ought to keep this promise (or help this person in need)', as one might say 'It so happens that the leaves of this tree are reddish-brown'. The moral judgement implies that making a promise necessarily carries an obligation to perform, that coming upon a person in need necessarily imposes a responsibility to help. The meaning of moral judgements commonly includes a necessity and a universality. To tell a particular person that he ought to do a particular action because he has promised is to imply that everyone always has an obligation to keep promises.

Always? Is it not sometimes right to break a promise? Yes, but only because of some other moral consideration which seems more important in the circumstances. I have promised to meet Mary at the theatre. As I am setting out, my next-door neighbour rushes up distraught and asks me to drive his wife to hospital: she has developed peritonitis; no ambulance is available just now, and no taxi either. Of course I should help. I should telephone Mary if I can, or get someone else to do so; but if it is too late to telephone Mary (she will already have left home), that is just too bad. I hope Mary will forgive me when she learns later what has happened.

When two moral principles conflict in a single situation, one of them has to give way. And since this can happen to *any* moral principles, it follows that no moral principle is universal in the sense of imposing a paramount duty on all occasions to which it applies. But even when a principle has to give way in a situation of conflict, it still retains moral force. In my example, the obligation to help my neighbour's wife is paramount, but this does not mean that my obligation to Mary simply has no force at all. If I can, I should let her know in time that I am not coming to meet her; if that is not possible, I am bound to feel some compunction at the knowledge that I am letting her down, and I must hasten to explain the situation to her as soon as I am in a position to do so.

Some rationalist philosophers (notably Immanuel Kant) have stressed the universal and necessary character of moral principles and have paid insufficient attention to conflicts between principles. Most, however, have appreciated that the universality of principles is qualified by the occurrence of conflict. But this does not weaken the rationalist's argument against the naturalist interpretation of moral judgements. The point is this: whether I ought to meet Mary at the theatre or to take the lady next door to hospital, in either case my obligation has a *rational ground*. I ought to meet Mary, or at least I ought to telephone her, because I promised; I ought to take the neighbour to hospital because she is ill and needs help. The judgement of what I ought to do is not a matter of my happening to feel warmly one way or the other.

Here, then, we have two alternative interpretations of moral judgement, two alternative philosophical positions, ethical naturalism and ethical rationalism. Debate between them in the eighteenth century centred on the question: is ethics a matter of feeling or reason? In the twentieth century more attention has been paid to the logical features of moral judgement. The old debate continues but it has taken on a new aspect, to be described in a new chapter.

3 Logic and language

Recent discussion of the difference between values and facts has concentrated on questions of logic and language. The eighteenth-century debate about reason and feeling was on a problem of epistemology but it looked like one of psychology. Philosophers of that time often wrote about the 'origin' of our moral ideas, as if they were giving a causal or genetic explanation. The same thing was true of general epistemological inquiry in the seventeenth and eighteenth centuries. The dispute between rationalism and empiricism about knowledge of the real world was often presented as if it were psychological, as if the question at issue were: Is knowledge the *causal result* of reason or sense-perception? In order to avoid this confusion, philosophers of the twentieth century have made a clear distinction between logical and psychological inquiry. Many of them have found it helpful to focus attention upon the language in which ideas are expressed, so as to get away from the habit of treating ideas as psychological entities open to direct inspection in consciousness. When one is considering the logical relation between ideas, one has to examine the ideas as expressed in words or other written symbols. This is one main reason why twentieth-century philosophy has spent so much of its time on language and especially on meaning. The old problems of epistemology have reappeared in a new guise. The spirit of eighteenth-century empiricism was revived in twentieth-century Logical Empiricism (or Logical Positivism). Earlier empiricism was a doctrine about knowledge; it held that genuine knowledge depends upon experience. The more recent Logical Empiricism or Positivism was a doctrine about meaning; it held that the meaning of a proposition (outside formal logic and pure mathematics) depends on the way in which it could be verified or falsified by experience.

So the debate in ethics between rationalism and naturalism has been continued in the twentieth century largely as an inquiry into the *meaning* of sentences expressing moral judgements. In this perspective, a simple naturalist theory would say that a moral judgement describes the feelings of the speaker. Suppose someone says 'Pulling the cat's tail (or, more generally, inflicting pain) is wrong'. What does he mean? If he says 'The cat's tail is long' he is describing a quality which we can see. The word 'wrong', unlike 'long', does not do that. Instead, the suggestion is, it describes the speaker's feeling of disapproval. The sentence 'Pulling the cat's tail is wrong' means the same as 'Pulling the cat's tail is disapproved by me' or 'I feel disapproval of pulling the cat's tail'. Let us call this suggestion the Individually Subjectivist Theory of the meaning of moral judgements.

We shall see a crucial weakness in this theory if we take an example about which there is liable to be a difference of opinion in moral judgement. Suppose Andrew and Barbara are discussing the possibility of reintroducing capital punishment. Andrew says 'Capital punishment is always wrong', and Barbara says 'Capital punishment is sometimes right' (e.g. for murders planned in cold blood, for the murder of a policeman, for hijacking). The individually subjectivist theory purports to tell us the meaning of any sentence of the form 'X is right' and 'X is wrong'. According to its analysis, Andrew's statement means 'I always disapprove of capital punishment', and Barbara's statement means 'I sometimes approve of capital punishment'. Now each of the second set of statements is autobiographical. Andrew tells us something about himself, Barbara tells us something about herself. There is *no contradiction* between the two statements. The same thing would be true if Andrew said 'I always take an egg for breakfast, and Barbara said 'I sometimes do not take an egg for breakfast'. There is no contradiction, no disagreement, between these two statements. Andrew and Barbara would simply be reporting bits of their autobiography in which they happen to differ. But when Andrew says 'Capital punishment is always wrong' and Barbara says 'Capital punishment is sometimes right', they both think that they are disagreeing in opinion, they think that Barbara has contradicted Andrew. They are likely to ask each other to give *reasons* for their opinions, and they will then see whether they agree or disagree on the reasons (e.g. that capital punishment has, or has not, a greater deterrent effect than alternative penalties), so as to find out whether this will help to resolve their disagreement on the initial question. Andrew and Barbara, then, think that their differing moral judgements express a difference of opinion and contradict each other. The analysis of their statements which is given by the subjectivist theory implies that they are not contradicting each other. The analysis has an implication not found in the original statements which it purports to analyse. So the analysis must be incorrect.

You may object that Andrew and Barbara are deluded in supposing that they disagree in opinion. In fact, you may say, they differ simply in their feelings, though we fail to understand this when we talk about these things in ordinary life. If so, the theory is true and cannot be rejected just because Andrew and Barbara, and indeed most of us, have failed to recognize its truth in our everyday experience.

But the theory claimed to tell us what it *means* to say 'X is right (or wrong)'. The meaning of a sentence is to be determined by its logical character and the circumstances of its use. If people actually use sentences of the form 'X is right', 'X is wrong', as contradictories of each other, it is no good saying that they are deluded and that the sentences cannot properly be used in that way. The proper use of a sentence is its actual normal use and the meaning of a sentence is to be gathered from its use. So 'X is right' cannot mean the same as 'I approve of X'. The individually subjectivist theory is false.

Can we do any better by making the theory less narrow? Let us modify it so as to claim that 'X is right' means 'Most people in my society approve of X'. We might call this modified version the Socially Subjectivist Theory of the meaning of moral judgements.

Well, this version runs into logical difficulties also. A person may hold a minority opinion on a moral issue, may know that his opinion is a minority view, and may still be convinced that his opinion is the morally sound one. He may say, for example, 'Euthanasia for those who want it is morally right, even though most people in my society disapprove of it'. Now the socially subjectivist theory tells us that the statement 'Euthanasia for those who want it is morally right' means the same as 'Most people in my society approve of euthanasia for those who want it'. According to this analysis, therefore, the complete statement of the minority-view holder means this: 'Most people in my society approve of euthanasia for those who want it, even though most people in my society disapprove of it.' That, of course, is a blatant self-contradiction. But the original statement which it purports to analyse was not in the least self-contradictory; the original statement made perfectly good sense. Consequently the socially subjectivist theory is just as faulty as the simpler individual version.

Ethical predicates, then, do not describe the feelings either of the speaker or of society at large. It seems clear that the meaning and the logical function of such expressions are not captured by saying that they describe feelings. Is there any other way in which ethical terms could be related to feelings?

The Expressive Theory,[1] held by Logical Positivists, gave a more subtle account in the hope of avoiding the logical difficulties of the

---

[1] A succinct version of the expressive theory is to be found in A.J. Ayer, *Language, Truth and Logic* (1936), chap.6. Sir Alfred Ayer calls it the Emotive Theory, and so do most other writers. I think this name is misleading because the subjectivist theory also gives an account of moral judgement in terms of emotion or feeling. The special feature of Ayer's theory is better described by the word 'expressive'.

subjectivist theory. According to this view, value judgements, including moral judgements, express or evince feelings. This is different from describing feelings. If I hit my thumb with a hammer and say 'Ow!' or something more colourful, I am expressing, evincing, giving vent to my feeling of pain. I am not describing it. I am not declaring 'I am in pain' or 'That is painful', though any spectator can infer from my exclamation that I am in pain. So if Caroline says 'Euthanasia (or capital punishment) is morally justifiable', she is not declaring that she has a feeling of approval but she is giving expression to such a feeling; and if David says 'Euthanasia is not morally justifiable', he is expressing a feeling of disapproval. Caroline and David are not describing their emotions, they are not indulging in bits of autobiography. They are, in a sense, contradicting, or at least opposing, each other, for they are expressing opposed attitudes. It is as if they were at a football match, supporting opposed teams. When Aston Villa scores a goal, Caroline cheers and David boos. According to this view, to say 'Euthanasia is right' is like shouting 'Hurrah for euthanasia!' and to say 'Euthanasia is wrong' is like shouting 'Boo to euthanasia!' Hence the expressive theory has also been called the Hurrah-Boo Theory.

Despite its ingenuity, the expressive theory does not avoid the difficulties which it tries to bypass. It is in fact subject to the same sort of objections as the subjectivist theory which it intends to replace. When people have and give voice to opposed views about the morality of capital punishment or euthanasia, they think that they differ in *opinion*, that statements of the form 'X is right' and 'X is wrong' literally *contradict* each other, and that they can argue about their views with *reasons*. Cheers and boos for Aston Villa are not regarded as statements of opinion which contradict each other or which can be supported by reasons. Suppose Aston Villa wins its game against Everton. David, who is a supporter of Everton, having finished booing, might say to Caroline: 'Well, Aston Villa won that game, but Everton is the better team all the same.' If Caroline disagrees that Everton is the better team, she and David will both think that now, in talking about 'the *better* team', they are differing in opinion and can back up their respective opinions with reasons. For instance, David points out that most of the game took place in Aston Villa's half of the field, that the one goal which was scored was just a bit of luck for Aston Villa because the Everton goalkeeper slipped, and so on. When Caróline and David differ on which is the better team, they do not behave as if they were simply cheering and booing.

So a straightforward comparison of value judgements with expressions of feeling cannot be correct. There are criteria or standards for applying value terms. The two football fans would perhaps agree on the criteria for calling a football team a good one: a good football team, they might both allow, is one which is fast, goes in for co-operative teamwork, and takes the initiative in attacking. And if they also both agreed, as they might, that Everton showed these qualities to a greater extent than Aston Villa, they would agree to call Everton the better team. Likewise people debating the merits of different motor-cars may reach broad agreement on the criteria for calling a car good: e.g. reliability, economy, comfort, fast acceleration. If a car meets these criteria, it is a good car. This kind of thing simply does not apply to shouting 'Ow!' when you hit your thumb with a hammer or to calling out 'Boo!' when a visiting football team scores a goal against the local one which you support.

The expressive theory could be modified in the following way. It could allow that particular value judgements depend on criteria or standards and so have an element of rationality; one can give reasons for saying that Everton is a good football team or that a Rover is a good car. But, the theory would now claim, the basic standards themselves are expressions of feeling. The two football fans can give reasons for and against the particular judgement that Everton is the better team, but not for and against the basic judgements which they use as standards or criteria: 'a fast team is a good one'; 'a team with attacking initiative is a good one'. Similarly, it would claim, we can give reasons for the particular judgement that the Rover is a good car, but not for the basic judgements of value which are used as standards for judging cars: 'a reliable car is a good one'; 'an economic car is a good one'. The basic judgements, which constitute reasons but which do not themselves depend on reasons, are, according to the modified theory, expressions of feeling.

But now the theory is telling us that *general* judgements ('Speed is good in a football team – *any* team'; 'Economy is good in a car – *any* car') are the expression of feelings, like a cry of pain at hitting one's thumb with a hammer. This analogy is quite ridiculous. The expression or evincing of such a feeling must be particular; it must refer to the here and now, to an individual case. Further, the analogue, crying out when you are hurt, is more or less involuntary. When I hit my thumb with a hammer, I may call out 'Ow!' willy-nilly; but if I give my reaction to painful situations *in general*, I cannot be evincing an involuntary cry. A liking for economy in a car goes along with a liking for economy in general, wanting to make your money stretch further. That is not a particular feeling.

The two types of theory which I have discussed so far, the subjectivist and the expressive theories, both claim that value judgements are non-rational. This claim does not hold water. We have seen that particular value judgements can be based on reasons and so are rational in that sense, while general value judgements must have an element of rationality in being general. It does not follow, however, that we must adopt a straightforward rationalist theory to the effect that general moral judgements are necessary truths, like the propositions of mathematics. This position, too, falls foul of a logical difficulty.

The rationalist theory takes values to be a kind of facts, not facts known by the experience of sense or feeling, but facts known by rational understanding. The fact that having your arm twisted is *painful* is something which we get to know by experience. The fact that pain is *bad* is, according to the rationalist, something which we get to know by rational understanding. Let us accept, for the sake of argument, that the proposition 'Pain is bad' states a fact. What then? We want to conclude that if pain is bad, we ought not to cause pain and we ought to remove pain when we are able. But how can we infer that we *ought* to do some action from the fact that something *is* somesuch? The inference would be fallacious because it would introduce into the conclusion a term which is not contained in the premisses. Compare these two simple syllogisms:

> All philosophers are *crackpots*.
> *Socrates* is a philosopher.
> Therefore: *Socrates* is a *crackpot*.

> All philosophers are crackpots.
> *Socrates* is a philosopher.
> Therefore: *Socrates* is *snub-nosed*.

In the first syllogism, which is logically valid (although one might doubt the truth of the first premiss, and so of the conclusion), both the subject and the predicate of the conclusion are terms which enter also into the premisses. In the second syllogism, however, the predicate of the conclusion introduces a term, 'snub-nosed', which was not included in either of the premisses. This syllogism is therefore logically invalid, although the conclusion happens to be true. Now the same sort of fallacy occurs in an inference in which the copula 'is' (or 'are') in the premisses is followed by the different type of copula 'ought' in the conclusion. For example:

> All pain *is* (or: all painful states *are*) bad.
> Starvation *is* painful.
> Therefore: Starvation *ought* to be alleviated.

It would be a valid inference if the conclusion were 'Starvation is bad', but to say that something is good or bad is not the same as saying that it ought to be produced or ought to be removed. If you say that *X* ought to be produced or ought to be done, you imply that *X* is not the case, is not a fact, now; you are talking about the possibility, and the urgency, of *making* something to be the case, to be a fact. And if you say that *Y* ought to be removed, you are talking about the possibility of making an existing fact cease to be one. A call to action cannot be simply a logical consequence of statements of fact.

This line of thought leads to a different sort of theory, Prescriptivism,[2] which concentrates on the practical character of the language of values. To say 'You ought to go to bed' is not exactly a command ('Go to bed') but it approaches a command. It is advice, recommendation, urging. Value judgements are not statements of what is the case. Nor are they simply expressions of what the speaker feels. They are exhortations to the hearer, intended to affect action. The older theories, both subjectivist and straightforward rationalist, compared value judgements with statements of fact. The expressive theory compared value judgements with exclamations. The prescriptive theory compares value judgements with commands.

So far as the word 'ought' is concerned, this seems plausible enough and is indeed nothing new. Kant, a rationalist of the eighteenth century, talked about moral judgements of 'ought' as 'imperatives'; he distinguished between the 'categorical imperative' of morality and the 'hypothetical imperatives' of prudence and of skill. Older theory still (that of Natural Law) compared moral principles with laws, which are generalized commands; and in the Old Testament fundamental moral principles are called 'Commandments' and are expressed in the imperative mood ('Honour thy father and thy mother'; 'Thou shalt not steal').

The prescriptive theory, as put forward by Professor Hare, also makes ample provision for the rational character of moral prescriptions. Hare, again reviving a key element of Kant's theory of ethics, has emphasized a feature of universality which, in his view, characterizes all moral judgements containing the word 'ought'. Such a moral judgement differs from a command proper, he says, precisely because it can be universalized. A command is normally addressed to a particular person or group and applies only to a particular situation. A moral prescription goes further; although it may say directly that a particular person is obliged to do this or that, it implies that anyone and everyone, in an exactly similar situation, would be likewise obliged.

What about value terms other than 'ought'? The adjectives 'right' and 'wrong' can be amalgamated with 'ought' and 'ought not'. A right action is one that ought to be done, a wrong action one that ought not to be done. 'Good' and 'bad', however, are rather different. They do not have quite such an obvious prescriptive force. The words 'right' and 'wrong', like 'ought' and 'ought not', are commonly applied to actions. 'Good' and

---

[2] See R.M. Hare, *The Language of Morals* (1952) and *Freedom and Reason* (1963).

'bad' are commonly applied to things and persons. We speak of a good knife, a good motor-car, a good football team, a good man. The prescriptive theory holds that the words 'good' and 'bad' are used, not to do something approaching a *command*, but instead to *commend* and *discommend*, and it interprets this as advising on choice. To say 'A Rover is a good car' is like saying 'If you want a car, choose a Rover'. When we use the word 'good' we assume broad agreement on the criteria to be applied to the satisfaction of a particular sort of desire: for a knife, sharpness; for a car, a range of things including reliability, economy, comfort. To say that a Rover is a good car is to advise choice of a Rover for the reason that it meets the criteria which most people have in mind when they want a car. The prescriptive theory's account thus allows both for the practical and for the rational character of the word 'good'.

It fits well enough when we speak of things that we use – motor-cars, knives, etc. But does it fit when we call a person good? Suppose I tell you about my friend John who has been so helpful and kind to me and to others when we were in trouble. I might say, to sum it up, 'He is a really good man'. I do not mean, by that remark, 'If you want a man, choose John' – as if I were addressing someone who was looking for a husband. When we praise human beings as morally good, we are not talking about use or function. To be sure, we can and often do talk about human beings as good in relation to a function. I might say of a successful politician that he would make a good Prime Minister, just as I might say of a piece of cloth that it would make a good mainsail. It is reasonable to treat both statements as having the same sort of meaning: 'If you want a new Prime Minister (mainsail), choose that politician (piece of cloth).' I might also use the *expression* 'good man' in relation to function. For example, if you are selecting a cricket team, I might say 'Jack Hobbs is a good man', meaning a good cricketer, so that here too my remark can be interpreted as advice to choose Jack Hobbs for your team. But when we speak of moral goodness, when I call John a good man because of his kindness, my commendation does not refer to a function and cannot be understood as advice to choose John for a function.

Hare deals with the difference between the functional and the moral senses of 'good' by treating the latter as advice for imitation instead of choice: to say that John is a good man is to urge one's hearers to take John as a model for their own action. But this suggestion has its difficulties. We may commend morally different styles of life that are not easily combined with each other,[3] in which case our commendation

[3] Cf. J.O. Urmson, 'Saints and Heroes', in A.I. Melden (ed.), *Essays in Moral Philosophy* (1958).

cannot well be understood as advice to all and sundry to take them as models for imitation. For example, we should think morally commendable the efforts of an Albert Schweitzer in devoting himself to the medical care of people suffering from leprosy in a backward country. We should also think morally commendable the efforts of a Winston Churchill in stirring his countrymen and their allies to maintain a long war against a monstrous tyranny. But it is hardly possible for any one person to combine the two styles of life, that of Schweitzer and that of Churchill. Again, I may know that some people are constitutionally incapable of becoming doctors, but that would not inhibit me from saying to them, as to others, that Albert Schweitzer was an exceptionally good man in what he did for lepers. No doubt this is to take too narrowly the idea that commendation of Schweitzer is urging one's listeners to imitate him: the imitation can be simply of his practical concern for people in need. But even allowing that, it seems to me that the prescriptive theory exaggerates the practical force of such commendation and neglects another aspect of it.

To see what this other aspect is, let us go back to one of our earlier examples. We can speak of a good football team as well as a good footballer. A good footballer, like a good car, is commended in relation to function, and the judgement that he is a good example of his kind may, in some circumstances (as when addressed to someone picking a football team), be understood to mean 'If you want another member of your football team, choose this man'. But in other circumstances one may call a man a good footballer without in the least suggesting that one's hearer is selecting a team or might want to do so in the future. Similarly, this kind of thing cannot be what was meant when our two football fans earlier agreed that Everton was a good football team. They did not mean 'If you want a football team, choose Everton'. We do not *use* football teams, as we use motor-cars and knives. We follow them and, if they are good, we admire them. If you are told that Everton is a good football team, or that its striker is a good footballer, you may take this to imply that if you want to watch a football match, you should choose to watch Everton and especially the Everton striker. But the actual appraisal of Everton or the striker as good is not giving that advice. It is expression admiration.

These examples are quasi-aesthetic, and it seems to me that aesthetic appraisal is more an expression of feeling than a giving of advice. Such expression of feeling, however, is not like a quasi-involuntary exclamation, as the expressive theory suggested. The feeling which it reflects is often based upon criteria (a football team is admired if it is fast, goes in for co-operative teamwork, takes the initiative in attacking), and when that is the case, the feeling is one which we can expect to be shared by many other people, though not necessarily by everyone.

The old analogy between ethics and aesthetics was not altogether mistaken. Moral appraisal of a person has something in common with aesthetic appraisal, especially aesthetic appraisal which rests on criteria. To call someone a morally good man is to express admiration of him – because of his traits of character and habits of action (i.e. because he possesses and practises virtues such as kindness, honesty, modesty, courage, etc.) – and it is also to imply that our feelings of admiration will be shared by everyone, or nearly everyone.

The upshot of this discussion is that value judgements differ from statements of fact in belonging to pragmatic, rather than descriptive, modes of language. They do not describe the world; they prescribe action or express reaction. This is not to say that they are irrational or non-rational. If traffic is approaching and I say 'Don't cross the road now', my advice is thoroughly rational. Prescriptions and appraisals which are based on reasons, and which can apply generally to a class of cases and to most persons, are properly called rational. They are not like arbitrary whims or unpredictable winces.

It will now be clear, I hope, that the linguistic approach to philosophical problems is neither trivial nor pointless. When the subjectivist theory confined itself to a simple definition of value terms as describing feelings of approval, this was indeed trivializing the force of naturalism. I rejected the theory on the ground that its logical implications ran counter to the logical implications of the normal usage of value terms. But although that was sufficient ground for rejecting subjectivism as a theory of the *meaning* of value terms, one was bound to be left with a sense of unease. Naturalism, as described in Chapter 2, clearly has a persuasive force, and one that is not dissipated by the refutation of a superficial theory like subjectivism. The refutation showed that in making moral judgements we do not mean, intend to state, that we have certain feelings. Nevertheless, if our meaning is taken to be an objectivist one, declaring that actions and situations actually possess a 'non-natural' or transcendental quality of rightness or goodness, why should we suppose that we are entitled to say any such thing? Perhaps we have been beguiled into using objectivist expressions when we have no warrant for doing so. Perhaps our ordinary thoughts and modes of utterance are illusory. The strength of this objection is brushed aside when one says that the subjectivist theory cannot be defended in this way because the subjectivist theory claims to tell us what we mean, not what we are entitled to mean. To that extent the linguistic exercises of the subjectivist theory are indeed trivial.

The expressive theory was hardly more convincing because its account of the function of evaluative language was also too simple. But the expressive theory did have the advantage of moving away from the fact-stating or descriptive mode of language to a more pragmatic mode. The point of such a move, however, comes out far more clearly in the prescriptive theory, which not only draws upon the analogue of imperative language but also makes provision for the rational character of much evaluative language. It allows for the persuasive features both of rationalism and of naturalism, while avoiding to a considerable degree (I do not say wholly) the objections made to them in their traditional form. It has been able to make this progress largely because it has focused upon the use and the logical implications of language.

The standard of morals

4 Utilitarianism

What is the standard of morals? What is it that makes right action right? One answer to this question is given by Utilitarianism. It is an attractive view and is deservedly popular. According to utilitarianism, an action is right if it is useful for promoting happiness. Happiness, the theory explains, is a sum of pleasures. Pleasure is good and pain or displeasure is bad. Actions are right if they produce what is good and remove or prevent what is bad; that is to say, if they produce happiness or pleasure and if they remove or prevent unhappiness or pain. More precisely, an action is right, the action which you ought to do, if it seems to you likely to produce the greatest possible amount of happiness, i.e. if it seems likely to produce more happiness, or to remove or prevent more unhappiness, than any alternative action available to you. A simple example can illustrate what is meant by this slight complication. If you can give pleasure to one child by taking him to the seaside, that is a good thing to do; but if you can give the same pleasure to two children, that is obviously better; so, as between the two possible actions, the second one would be right, the action which you ought to do.

There is a form of utilitarianism which says that pleasure or happiness is not the only thing which is good in itself. According to this version of the theory, other good things are virtue, love, knowledge (or truth), and beauty. Traditional utilitarianism, which tries to simplify things as much as possible, says that pleasure is the sole intrinsic good and that these other things are valued for the sake of pleasure, either the pleasure which they themselves contain or the pleasure which they are likely to produce. We need to make a distinction between good as a means and good as an end. If something is valued for its own sake, it is good as an end, intrinsically good. But if a thing is valued for the sake of something else which it produces, then it is good as a means. For example, good coffee is coffee that is enjoyable, pleasant, good as an end; a good coffee percolator is one that makes good coffee, it is good as a means, useful for producing something which is good for its own sake. The difference becomes clearer when one reflects that a thing may be useful, good as a means, for producing a bad end as well as a good end. A good thumbscrew is one that really makes its victims shriek; it is good (efficient) for producing pain instead of pleasure.

Utilitarianism of all varieties says that right actions are useful actions, good as means; that rightness is in fact a kind of efficiency, but restricted to efficiency for good ends. Screwing down the thumbscrews is a good (efficient) way of giving pain, but its efficiency or utility for *that* purpose does not make it right. Right acts are acts which are useful, efficient, for good purposes or ends. Classical utilitarianism says that the only purpose which counts is the production of pleasure or happiness and the removal or prevention of pain or unhappiness; it is the only purpose which counts because pleasure and pain are the only things good and bad as ends, good and bad in themselves. Classical utilitarianism is often called Hedonistic Utilitarianism (from *hedone*, the Greek word for pleasure) because it holds that pleasure alone is good as an end. The form of utilitarianism which says that other things besides pleasure (virtue, love, knowledge, beauty) are good as ends is called Ideal Utilitarianism. Both forms are called utilitarian because they both maintain that the only reason for an act to be right is its utility, its usefulness for producing results which are good in themselves.

Hedonistic utilitarianism agrees that virtue, love, knowledge, and beauty are good, but it denies that their goodness is independent of the goodness of pleasure. It says that they are good either because they are enjoyable (pleasant) or because they are a means to pleasure. Let us see how the argument goes for each of the four.

First, virtue. Virtue or moral goodness can take either of two forms. One is the habit or disposition of doing the right thing because it is right, of acting from a sense of duty. The second form is the habit or disposition of acting from certain other admired motives such as kindness, pity, courage. Hedonistic utilitarianism says that both types of disposition are good as means. It has already told us that right actions are valued as means, valued for their utility. The habit or disposition to act from a sense of duty, to do right actions because they are right, is likewise useful because it prompts us to do these right (i.e. useful) actions. Virtuous motives other than the sense of duty are useful in the same sort of way. Motives like kindness, pity, and courage are valued because they aim at giving pleasure or removing pain and danger of pain. A kind person is one who tries to benefit other people, to give them pleasure. Pity prompts us to help those in distress, to remove pain or unhappiness. Courage is a readiness to run risks for the sake of preventing danger. The fireman goes into a burning house in order to save people trapped inside. The bomb-disposal expert risks his life in order to prevent harm to others. If there is no danger from a fire, if there are no people to be saved or no valuables to be rescued, there is no virtue in rushing into the burning house just to show that you are capable of facing something nasty. The value of virtue, says the hedonistic utilitarian, lies in its utility for increasing happiness or decreasing unhappiness. To sacrifice your own happiness when there is no prospect of producing a greater happiness for others is not admirable but foolhardy – indeed, strictly speaking, it is wrong, for it is to diminish happiness unnecessarily. The same proviso applies to the first form of virtue, acting from the sense of duty. There is nothing admirable in a pointless sense of duty which makes a St. Simeon Stylites spend his life sitting on the top of a pillar just to show that he can endure it. Still less is there anything admirable in the perverted sense of duty of a fanatic like Hitler, which drives him to bring immeasurable misery to millions of people for the sake of a crazy ideal.

Next, take the example of love. Love is valued, according to hedonistic utilitarianism, both for the happiness that it contains and for the happiness that it produces as a consequence. Love is itself a happy state of mind and it acts as a motive to produce happiness for the loved one. There is no need to think of its value as something separate from the value of happiness.

Thirdly, knowledge. The value attached to the pursuit of knowledge or truth is again derivative, in these two ways, from the value of happiness. Most knowledge, though not all, is useful in adding to happiness, and the search for knowledge is itself enjoyable for many people because it satisfies the natural human trait of curiosity. Sometimes the pursuit of knowledge, like the display of courage, is not useful. If it is quite clear that a particular piece of knowledge would not be useful and would give little satisfaction to the inquirer, a hedonistic utilitarian would say that such knowledge is not valuable, it is trivial rubbish. The ideal utilitarian, who holds that knowledge is good in itself, is committed to placing a value on the pursuit of all knowledge, whatever its character. The doctrine sounds admirable when one thinks of research into the causes and cure of cancer, and quite feasible when one thinks of the excitement of useless but enjoyable discoveries made in pure mathematics or history; but much less plausible when one reads of some plodding piece of 'research' which is of no significance to the researcher or anybody else, undertaken simply because the idea of research has become fashionable. The hedonistic utilitarian would have no hesitation in condemning such inquiry as worthless.

Finally there is the value of beauty, that is to say, of the appreciation and creation of beauty. Hedonistic utilitarianism says that the value of aesthetic appreciation lies simply in the fact that it is an enjoyable experience. The value of aesthetic creation has a twofold character; it is both enjoyable (usually, though not always) to the artist who is engaged in it, and it tends to be useful because it aims at giving aesthetic enjoyment to potential spectators or audiences.

Hedonistic utilitarianism thus makes quite a persuasive case for the view that the value of 'ideal' goods really rests on the value of pleasure. The argument is not foolproof and can be challenged at certain points. In the case of virtue, for example, it implies that unhappiness for Hitler's victims could have been compensated by a greater amount of happiness for others; and in the case of beauty, it implies that the music of Beethoven can properly be called better than that of the Beatles only if it gives more pleasure. On the other hand, the robust dismissal of the value of a perverted conscience, pointless self-sacrifice, and trivial knowledge strikes me as more sensible than the view of ideal utilitarianism that every exercise of a virtuous motive and every piece of knowledge are intrinsically good. There are further reasons for taking classical hedonistic utilitarianism more seriously than the ideal version. The classical utilitarians always treated their theory of ethics as a basis for legal and social reform, while most (not all) of the supporters of ideal utilitarianism concentrated on personal and aesthetic values, regarding practical social consequences as too remote for any firm pronouncements on their part. So, in order to proceed with expounding the position of classical hedonistic utilitarianism, I am going to assume (though in fact I do not believe) it can sustain its view that the only thing good in itself is pleasure and that all other good things are to be valued either because they contain pleasure or because they are a means to pleasure.

We next need to ask whose pleasure is to count, and the answer given by classical utilitarianism is anybody's and everybody's. Not just human pleasure either. From all appearances, many animals seem capable of experiencing pleasure and certainly of suffering pain. According to hedonism, pleasure is good and pain is bad wherever they occur. To be sure, the actions of one individual are not going to have any significant effect on the happiness of every creature in the world, and utilitarianism does not require a person to take account of all infinitesimal consequences of his possible acts. The theory tells me that, in deciding what I ought to do, I must take account of the likely consequences for the happiness and unhappiness of all persons, and other creatures, who will be significantly affected. I am not required to think about possible minute, indirect effects upon the condition of people at the other side of the earth.

It is often said that the classical utilitarians took the view that everyone does, as a matter of fact and psychological necessity, always have as his constant motive of action a concern for his *own* maximum happiness.

Jeremy Bentham, the acknowledged leader of the classical utilitarians in the nineteenth century, did sometimes write as if this were so, but I think his opinion really was that people *usually* act from the motive of self-interest, not that they always do. There were some writers before Bentham who thought they could combine an egoistic psychology with a utilitarian ethic. They have held (1) that as a matter of psychological fact every human being does and must necessarily act so as to maximize his own happiness, and (2) that as a matter of ethical principle every person ought to act so as to maximize the general happiness. A simple combination of these two positions would be inconsistent. The second proposition, which says that everyone ought to act with the purpose of maximizing the general happiness, implies that it is possible for us to act from a disinterested motive, taking the general happiness, not our own, as our end. The first proposition, however, implies that we can never act from a disinterested motive but must always be moved by self-interest. I do not know of any utilitarian who in fact adopted this inconsistent position (often attributed to Bentham). Utilitarians who definitely held an egoistic psychology usually took care to avoid the inconsistency by denying that action to promote the general happiness would be disinterested. They said that a prudent man would realize that he needs the help of others to achieve his own maximum happiness and that he should induce their help by doing things for them. That is to say, these philosophers took the ethical principle, everyone ought to act so as to maximize the general happiness, to be a principle of prudence: everyone ought to do that as a necessary means to his ultimate purpose of maximizing his own happiness. This implies that the ethical principle, 'one *ought* to promote the general happiness', really means that one necessarily will do so if the inevitable motive of self-interest is guided by prudential understanding of how best to secure one's interest.

Some utilitarians avoided the inconsistency in a different way, with a theory which may be called Theological Utilitarianism. On this view, the promotion of the general happiness is the purpose of God, who does not suffer from the limitations of human nature in being self-interested. Although disinterested benevolence is psychologically impossible for men, it is an essential part of the nature of God. He arranges for his disinterested purpose to be served by self-interested human beings through setting before them the prospect of reward or punishment for obeying or disobeying his commands. The commands themselves are designed to bring about God's purpose of making all his creatures happy. Moral obligation, on this view, is again prudential. A man ought to obey the will of God in the same sense as he ought to follow the precepts of his doctor; it will be better for him if he does and worse for him if he does not.

Both the secular and the theological versions of this combination of egoistic psychology and a utilitarian standard of ethics were held by some writers in the eighteenth century; but they were not in the main stream of utilitarianism. Leading utilitarians, before and after Bentham, have taken the view that men are capable of acting from disinterested as well as from interested motives. They have argued that we reach the utilitarian standard of morality, promotion of the general happiness, either from a simple benevolence or through the operation of sympathy with the needs and desires of others.

In Chapter 2 I wrote of two kinds of naturalism, one relying on an egoistic account of human nature, the other relying on an account which highlighted sympathy. These two varieties of naturalism have now reappeared in what I have said about utilitarianism, but this does not mean that there is a necessary connection between naturalism and utilitarianism. There have been plenty of naturalists in ethical theory who have taken an egoistic view of human nature but have not subscribed to a utilitarian standard of ethics. There have been some non-egoistic naturalists who have combined an emphasis on benevolence or on sympathy in their view of human psychology with opposition to utilitarianism in their account of the standards of ethics. There has also been one very distinguished hedonistic utilitarian (Henry Sidgwick) who rejected naturalism, as an inadequate basis for ethics. Neverthelesss it remains true as a broad generalization that the main stream of utilitarianism has accepted naturalism, and (in my understanding of the history of the subject) naturalism in its non-egoistic form.

This is not to say that such utilitarians take a starry-eyed view of altruism in human nature. There was a good reason for Bentham and others to stress the prevalence of self-interest. The motive of self-interest affects utilitarianism when the theory considers the relation of ethics to law and government. The nineteenth-century utilitarians (Bentham and his followers, especially James Mill, John Stuart Mill, John Austin) were very much concerned with the social and political implications of ethics, and particularly with the role of the legal system. They were reformers; they were known as the Philosophical Radicals; they used their philosophical theory of ethics as the basis of a programme of legal and social reform. They held that the standard of morally right action is the increase of happiness (or the decrease of unhappiness) as much as possible for as many people as possible – 'the greatest happiness of the greatest number'. But while men can follow an ethical standard in some of their conduct in private life, it is foolish to expect this of them in action which affects the life of society. For the most part, most people act with a view to their own happiness, to self-interest. The chief concern of utilitarianism is to explain that the function of law and government is to match up the two things, self-interested motivation and the effective pursuit of the ethical standard. It is wise to assume that men do generally act so as to serve their own advantage: how then can their actions be made to serve the advantage of everyone, or at least of most people?

In the field of economics, the classical utilitarians of the nineteenth century followed Adam Smith in thinking that there was a *natural* harmony of interests. Although each person in economic life aims at his own advantage, the net result is the best possible advantage for society as a whole. Governmental interference in the economy disturbs this natural harmony and results in less efficiency, a lesser total national product. So the recipe for economics was *laissez-faire*, leave well alone, no governmental interference, complete liberty. Few people would say that now. Even the USA, the freest of national economies today, has some governmental control over part of the economy, e.g. in monetary policy, in using taxation partly for the redistribution of income by way of welfare benefits for the unemployed and for old-age pensioners, and in things vital to defence such as nuclear armaments and outer-space technology. But there are still plenty of economists who believe that in general the utilitarians were right and that governmental interference in the economy does more harm than good. For example, it is commonly said by most economists that in communist States, where pretty well everything in economic life is controlled by the government, the economy is less efficient than that of a capitalist country. And lots of people, whether economists or laymen, will argue that in Britain the nationalization of the mines, the railways, and the electricity and gas industries resulted in less efficiency because of the absence of competition. However, these are matters on which any opinion worthy of respect requires a knowledge of economic facts. I simply note that the classical utilitarians happened to take a *laissez-faire* view of economics, though this is not necessitated by their philosophy. They took that view on grounds of economic theory.

So far as other aspects of social life are concerned, the utilitarians thought that there was not a natural harmony of interests. In fact the whole point of having a system of law and government is that, without a system of control, there is a conflict of interests. The purpose of government is to produce an *artificial* harmony of interests. How? By means of the system of law.

The primary purpose of law is to protect person and property. Murder, assault, theft, fraud – indeed all crimes – are harmful to individuals and to society at large: they diminish the stock of happiness directly in their immediate victims, and also indirectly by causing a fear of like danger to others. Such actions are commonly done for the sake of individual gain. A thief steals in order to benefit himself. What is harmful to society can seem attractive to the individual. Here is a familiar instance of a divergence between individual and social interests.

Now if we must count on the behaviour of the individual (the would-be thief) as being motivated by self-interest, the way to harmonize that with the benefit of society is to make unattractive to the individual the action which he now finds attractive. The thief is attracted by the prospect of obtaining pleasure with the money which he steals. But the prospect of imprisonment makes the whole enterprise unattractive. The criminal law adds the prospect of unpleasantness and so deters the would-be thief from doing an action which is harmful to society. The law, with its sanctions (punishments and other penalties), makes an artificial harmony of private and public interest. It gives the potential criminal a motive for not doing socially harmful actions; it makes such actions unattractive (unpleasant) to him as well as to society.

The main business of government is to secure the interest (the happiness) of society by making and administering laws. Laws get their effectiveness from sanctions – imprisonment, fines, requirement to compensate. The utilitarian theory is that laws exist to promote the happiness of the community; the sanctions of law help this cause by making socially harmful action unattractive to those who would otherwise be attracted to do it. The theory has a beautiful simplicity. It gives one, simple, general criterion of morally right action, and it uses the same simple principle as the rationale of government and law.

In its bare essentials the theory is a secularized version of theological utilitarianism. According to theological utilitarianism, God has a beneficent purpose, the happiness of his creation, and induces incorrigibly self-interested human beings to serve that beneficent purpose by the promise of reward in heaven for obedience to his commands and by the threat of punishment in hell for disobedience. According to secular utilitarianism, government has (or should have) a beneficent purpose, the greatest happiness of the greatest number, and induces individuals, who are largely though not entirely self-interested, to serve the general interest by the threat of earthly punishment for disobedience to its laws.

But secular utilitarianism has more to say than that. It implies a relatively mild, not a severe, penal system and so it is conducive to law reform. Sanctions are used because they threaten something painful or unpleasant – prison, a fine, social disgrace. According to utilitarianism, anything painful or unpleasant is bad. The unpleasantness of punishment is justifiable only as a *necessary* evil, necessary to prevent a still greater evil, harm to the victim of the crime and to society generally. But if punishment is an evil, then it should be no greater than is necessary. If a crime, a socially harmful act, can be prevented by a lesser punishment, it would be wrong to use one which is greater than necessary, for that would mean producing more pain in the total result than is essential. So if a would-be sheep stealer will be deterred as effectively by a threat of imprisonment for three months as by a threat of hanging (the prescribed penalty in Bentham's day) or as by a threat of imprisonment for six months, then the lesser punishment not only can but *ought* to be adopted. On the utilitarian theory it would be morally wrong to inflict the more severe penalty.

According to utilitarianism, the whole system of legal justice is a matter of utility. So is the very idea of justice. Utilitarianism regards punishment as a matter of deterrence. An alternative theory of punishment (the retributive theory) maintains that the notion of *just desert* has to come in: punishment is warranted because it is deserved, it is to be inflicted for what has been done in the past, not (or at least not only) for its consequences in preventing harm in the future. Utilitarianism replies that justification in terms of desert does not really bring in any argument different from utility, for desert depends on utility. We say that a man deserves reward for doing good (i.e. that he ought to be given a benefit for having conferred a benefit) because he has done what is useful and because the reward is useful in encouraging him and others to carry on the good work. Similarly we say that a man deserves punishment for wrongdoing (i.e. that he ought to be pained for having done harm) because what he has done is contrary to utility and because the punishment is useful in discouraging him and others from doing harm in the future. Justice, like other virtues, is valued for its utility.

It will be seen that utilitarianism is both comprehensive and simple. It uses a simple standard with an obvious appeal – promoting happiness for as many people as possible – in order to explain and link together ethics, law, and government. It is a forward-looking doctrine, justifying things by reference to the future, and so it seems clearly to be a progressive policy. No wonder that it captures the imagination as a most attractive moral philosophy.

5 Intuitionism and objections to utilitarianism

Despite its attractions, utilitarianism is faced with severe difficulties. I shall approach these by first considering the most obvious alternative to utilitarianism. This is a theory commonly called Intuitionism. It has usually been held by rationalist philosophers who have talked of reaching moral judgements by the exercise of rational 'intuition' or understanding. Utilitarians have claimed that intuitionism is defective and that their own theory remedies the defects.

Intuitionism says that there are several principles of right action, each of these principles serving as the standard or criterion of one class of right acts or duties. The principles, it maintains, are self-evident, known to be true by rational intuition. The word 'intuition', so used, has nothing to do with the idea of intuition as an inexplicable hunch (when, for example, people talk of women's intuition). It simply means understanding. It comes from a Latin word which originally meant looking at something and was then used metaphorically of intellectual 'seeing', just as the words 'grasp' and 'apprehend' have been transferred from the idea of a physical to that of an intellectual act. Rationalist philosophers used the word 'intuition' first for the understanding of self-evident truths in logic and mathematics, including the self-evident necessity by which a conclusion follows from the premises of a deductive inference. Some of them applied the word to the understanding of moral principles, claiming that these were strictly analogous to the self-evident truths of logic and mathematics. This does not mean that moral principles are blindingly obvious to any child. As with mathematical truths, we first become aware of them by teaching, but once we have reached maturity of understanding, it is claimed, we can see for ourselves that they are plainly true. The later attitude is not simply the result of conditioning, for we do not come to regard as self-evident *all* the moral rules which were taught to us by our parents or by religious doctrine. Some of those rules change from one generation to another, rules about the moral standing of marriage and divorce, for instance, or the Victorian rule that children should be seen and not heard. Rules which do not change from generation to generation, but acquire the character of necessary principles, cannot owe that character to doctrinal teaching.

Which moral rules, then, are self-evident principles? Intuitionists will tell you that the principles prescribe all or most of the following categories of action.

(1) Promoting the happiness of other people.

(2) Refraining from harm to other people.

(3) Treating people justly (which might mean either (*a*) in accordance with merit, or (*b*) equally, or (*c*) in accordance with need).

(4) Telling the truth (or, more accurately, refraining from deceit, for it would be an absurd imposition on other people, not a moral obligation to them, to tell them every truth that we happen to know).

(5) Keeping promises (including the fulfilment of contracts, e.g. the payment of debts, since the obligation to do so arises from promises).

(6) Showing gratitude.

(7) Promoting one's own happiness (prudence).

(8) Maintaining and promoting one's own virtues (self-respect).

There is a certain lack of clarity in this list of what is alleged to be self-evident. Not all intuitionists cite every one of these principles or classify them in the same way. For example, some deny that prudence (no. 7 in my list) is a moral duty – except as a necessary means to carrying out actions which are moral duties in themselves. Others go further and say this about self-respect also. Some put together (1) and (2), promoting happiness and avoiding unhappiness for other people. Some again put together (1), (2), and (7), thereby producing the utilitarian principle of promoting happiness and avoiding unhappiness for all, including oneself. There is much difference of opinion in the interpretation of justice: some say that merit is the essential criterion for justice; others that it is need; yet others that it is equality. Is gratitude a separate principle or is it simply an application of the principle of justice which says that merit should be requited? Are truth-telling and promise-keeping separate principles? One intuitionist says that truth-telling is a form of promise-keeping because there is a tacit promise in communication between man and man to use language so as to convey the truth and not deceive. Another intuitionist makes the reverse claim that the more fundamental principle is truth-telling (non-deceit) and that the keeping of promises is a form of this because breaking a promise is a deceit; it turns the promise into a lie.

Despite a lack of unanimity on the details of their list of principles, intuitionists are agreed in their criticism of utilitarianism. The defect of utilitarianism is that it selects a couple of the most important principles and neglects the rest. It selects the principles which look to future consequences and neglects those which depend on the past (justice in accordance with merit, promise-keeping, gratitude) and those whose force has nothing to do with time (truth-telling, the equality and the needs concepts of justice).

Intuitionism is itself criticized (by utilitarians and others) on two main counts. Most philosophers agree that intuitionism, with its list of several principles or standards of right action, gives an accurate picture of the way in which moral judgements are generally reached in ordinary life. But, they continue, that is not enough for a satisfactory theory.

(i) The first objection is that, on the intuitionists' own showing, the principles are not self-evident, or at least not all of them are. If they really were self-evident, they would not be subject to the lack of clarity and the disagreement which come out of the different accounts given by different intuitionists. No doubt the lack of clarity reflects a vagueness in the moral consciousness of ordinary life, but one of the tasks of a philosophical theory is to remove such vagueness, to make clear what lies below the surface of everyday moral thought.

(ii) The second objection has a practical as well as a theoretical purpose. If your moral scheme of things contains more than one principle or standard, you can be faced with a conflict. For example, you may find yourself in a situation where you can keep a promise only at the expense of sacrificing some happiness (of others or of yourself); or you may find that you can give a truthful answer to a question only at the expense of breaking a promise of confidentiality. When two moral principles conflict in this way, one of them has to go by the board. That one, therefore, cannot be a self-evident principle in the sense of being necessary and *universal*; if it has to give way to the conflicting principle, it does not apply as a principle of duty in this situation. Furthermore, intuitionism supplies no criterion for resolving the conflict. What we need, the objection continues, is a *single fundamental* principle which underlies the common rules of ordinary moral thinking and which we can use for decision in cases of conflict. Intuitionism accurately describes the common rules of ordinary moral thinking, but it fails to tell us what single principle underlies them all and can therefore arbitrate between them when necessary.

According to utilitarianism, the greatest happiness principle serves that function. It underlies all the common rules listed by the intuitionists. Rules (1), (2), and (7) in my list (promoting happiness for others and for oneself, and avoiding harm) are each a part of the greatest happiness principle. The other common rules have grown up because of their utility as means to the end of promoting general happiness. We saw at the conclusion of Chapter 4 that utilitarianism treats justice as a matter of utility; the rules of justice are adopted because they are useful. Utilitarianism takes the same view of the rules of truth-telling, promise-keeping, gratitude, and self-respect. All these things are useful and that is why they have become common rules of morality, rules of what we normally ought to do. Since all these rules have grown up because the actions which they prescribe are generally the most useful ones we can do, we do not need to work out the utility for ourselves in every instance. In most situations we can simply follow the particular common rule which applies. But when we are faced with a situation where two such rules conflict, we must refer back to the fundamental principle of utility which underlies them all. In a case of conflict we must think out for ourselves which of the alternative actions will do most to promote general happiness or diminish general unhappiness.

The two objections to intuitionism have considerable force. Utilitarianism aims to provide a way of escape from them. Does it in fact do so?

(i) The first objection was to the alleged self-evidence of the principles of intuitionism. What about the principle of utility itself? Is that self-evident, and if it is not, how is it reached? Two or three utilitarians have argued that the principle of utility is self-evident. Everyone agrees that it is right to increase happiness as much as possible. There is no dispute about it; clearly it is self-evident. But the matter is not altogether clear. It is not universally agreed that making oneself happy is on all fours with making other people happy. We all naturally *want* happiness for ourselves and we shall all naturally pursue it. There is certainly nothing *wrong* in promoting one's own happiness. But is it a *moral duty*, exactly on a par with making other people happy? Since there is doubt and disagreement about that, i.e. about the intuitionists' principle of prudence as a principle of moral duty, there must be doubt about the greatest happiness principle of the utilitarians, the principle that our moral duty is to maximize the happiness of everyone who may be affected, ourselves equally with others. The principle is as much subject to uncertainty as the intuitionists' principle of prudence. It is not unambiguously self-evident.

Other utilitarians, however, want nothing to do with self-evidence in asking us to accept the principle of utility. Rationalists, including intuitionists, think of self-evident truths, whether in logic and mathematics or in ethics, as a species of genuine knowledge about the world acquired simply by rational understanding. The utilitarians who want nothing to do with self-evidence are empiricists in the theory of knowledge and therefore naturalists in ethical theory. They believe that genuine knowledge about the world always depends on the experience of sense or feeling. The truths of logic and mathematics do not give us new information about the world; they are necessary and universal because they depend on definition and man-made rules of language or symbols; they are, in a sense, tautologies. The principle of utility is not at all like that. Utilitarians regard it as certainly a piece of genuine knowledge, and the empiricist (or naturalist) utilitarians argue that we acquire it from the experience of feeling. They say that while we instinctively feel warmly towards our own happiness and want to promote it, we come to have similar feelings towards the happiness of others through the operation of sympathy. The different psychological mechanisms which lead us to pursue the one and the other explain the somewhat different attitudes which we have towards the promotion of our own happiness and the promotion of the happiness of others. What these utilitarians have not made clear, however, is how they themselves can go on from these positive psychological facts to make the normative judgement that it is rational or right to regard all happiness, whether one's own or that of other people, in the same light.

(ii) The second objection to intuitionism concerned the possibility of conflict between principles. Utilitarianism claims to provide one underlying principle to be used as a criterion in resolving conflicts. But does utilitarianism really give us a single principle? It tells us that the right action is that which produces the greatest happiness for the greatest numbers. The criterion has two components: it urges us to *produce* as *much* happiness as possible, and to *distribute* it as *widely* as possible. There are two principles here, not one, and they can conflict. Suppose that I have £40 to give away. Should I give £20 to each of two old-age pensioners, perhaps enabling each of them to buy a cardigan which will help to keep them warm over the winter? Or should I give 20p to each of two hundred pensioners, enabling each of them to do something like buying a cup of tea? It seems to me that the results of the first action add up to a greater total of happiness produced, but of course only two people are affected, as against the two hundred who would be benefited by the second action. Which of the alternatives am I supposed to choose if I use the principle of utility as my guide?

The so-called principle of utility or greatest happiness principle is in fact a principle of utility plus a principle of justice; it is a principle of aggregation plus a principle of distribution. The second part of it adopts an egalitarian concept of justice: in Bentham's words, 'everybody to count for one, nobody for more than one'.

The most difficult moral conflicts, especially in social life, are conflicts between utility and justice. A common example keeps on occurring in fiscal and wages policy: should government adopt a policy which would provide incentives to maximize the gross national product, the total means to happiness in the community as a whole, or should it adopt a policy which would redistribute income and wealth so as to produce greater fairness? All political parties attach value to both these objectives, but conservatives give more emphasis to the first while socialists give more emphasis to the second. Another example can be found in education policy: should a government provide larger grants for students of engineering 'in the national interest' or should government grants for students be the same in all subjects for the sake of fairness? Again, in countries which have conscription for the armed forces, should the call-up be selective so as not to deprive vital industries or professions of key workers, or should it apply indiscriminately to all fit men so as to avoid injustice? These are all real conflicts between the two separate principles of utility and justice. No one has produced a single concept which embraces both or can adjudicate between them. Utilitarianism blurs the recurring conflict, having deceived itself into thinking that it has a single principle. Intuitionism, with its greater number of moral principles, has to face a wider variety of conflicts. To this extent utilitarianism represents an improvement. But since the major conflicts of social life are those between utility and justice, the improvement does not go far towards removing the problem.

Utilitarianism, then, does not altogether clear the first hurdle which faced intuitionism, and undoubtedly falls at the second one. In addition, however, the particular character of the utilitarian theory makes it liable to some further objections.

(iii) The so-called principle of utility, I have said, also includes a principle of distributive justice. When including justice in the list of principles given by intuitionists, I said that this can be interpreted as requiring equal distribution, or distribution according to merit, or distribution according to need. The utilitarian formula includes an egalitarian principle of justice, everyone to be treated equally. What about the other two concepts of distributive justice? The needs concept of justice in fact goes together with the egalitarian concept, as we shall see in Chapter 7. The merit concept, however, is different. Utilitarianism says that utility underlies the merit principle of justice. Conduct which is praised as meritorious and therefore deserving of reward is socially useful action; it is commended because it is useful, and it is rewarded because reward is useful in encouraging people to do the kind of socially useful action which is singled out in this way. Conversely, conduct which is reproved as having demerit is socially harmful action, and when it is punished the justification for inflicting the unpleasantness of punishment is that punishment is useful in deterring the wrongdoer and other potential wrongdoers from committing socially harmful acts.

But this utilitarian account of punishment would occasionally justify the 'punishment' of the innocent. Here is a hypothetical example, not too far-fetched. Let us suppose that planted bombs in London have become a menace. (It has happened from time to time as an offshoot of the troubles in Northern Ireland.) The police find circumstantial evidence which points to Paddy O'Connor as one of those concerned. He is, or used to be, a member of the IRA. He was seen with a brown-paper parcel at Harrods on the day when a bomb went off there. He is charged with having planted it. During the course of the trial the police discover some new evidence which shows that Paddy's story of a harmless parcel was true after all. But the defence have not learned of the new evidence and it could safely be kept dark. The police have had very little success in dealing with the present wave of bomb attacks. If Paddy is convicted and is given an 'exemplary' heavy sentence, that seems likely to have some deterrent effect on genuine bombers belonging to the IRA, for they have no reason to suspect the sincerity of the police; they will know that if anyone else is caught on apparently incriminating evidence, he too will be given a long sentence of imprisonment. The police can therefore conclude that it will be useful to have Paddy convicted. On the utilitarian theory it will be right for them to get Paddy convicted. Yet surely it is wrong to convict an innocent man, however useful it might be; it is wrong for the police to allow the conviction of a man who they now think is innocent, even though they also think that the conviction would be useful in having a deterrent effect. Useful or not, conviction for alleged crime is justified only if the person charged is guilty of the crime.

Perhaps you are unimpressed by a hypothetical example, unlikely ever to be realized in this country because of the traditions instilled into the police. Then consider instead real-life examples of conviction, with no deliberate cover-up by the police, on evidence which later came to be thought suspect or inadequate. In 1950 a man named Timothy Evans gave the police an apparently convincing confession that he had murdered his wife. Later the police obtained statements from two witnesses which cast doubt on Evans's version of how he had disposed of the body, but the police assumed that the witnesses were mistaken, persuaded them to amend their statements, and did not make the original statements available to the defence. Evans was convicted and hanged. Some years later it came out that a neighbour was the real murderer. In 1908 a man named Oscar Slater was convicted of murder on evidence which was considered, twenty years afterwards, to have been inadequate. Fortunately (relatively speaking) Slater had not been hanged, the capital sentence having been commuted in his case to life imprisonment; but that was bad enough. In these cases there was no deliberate malpractice on the part of the authorities; the miscarriage of justice was a genuine mistake. One may doubt whether capital punishment or life imprisonment does in fact do much to deter potential murderers. However, if such punishment does deter, it will do so where there is a general honest *belief* that convicted persons are guilty. So the deterrent effect of the conviction of a Timothy Evans or an Oscar Slater depends on the belief that they are guilty. When those two men were convicted, there was an honest belief of that kind, the result of apparently sound evidence. In those circumstances the convictions would have had as much deterrent effect on potential murderers as would the convictions of genuinely guilty murderers. Therefore, according to utilitarianism, the convictions of Timothy Evans and of Oscar Slater were quite justified.

This is not to say that utilitarianism would countenance slackness in testing the evidence against persons charged with murder or any other crime. When it becomes known that an innocent person can be mistakenly convicted, the deterrent effect of punishment is blunted; for a potential criminal may say to himself that he has some chance of being convicted whether or not he commits an offence and so he might as well go for the benefit of the crime. His thought is irrational, of course, since the chances of conviction when innocent are still incomparably smaller than when guilty. But still it remains true that the discovery of wrongful convictions takes the edge off deterrence. Yet if the mistake is not discovered and is unlikely to be discovered, all is well – on the utilitarian theory. The deterrent effect is undamaged; what is there to worry about?

What there is to worry about is injustice to an individual. Utilitarianism implies that the injustice of executing Timothy Evans and imprisoning Oscar Slater consists in the decrease of general security at the later date when the mistake became known. It is nothing of the kind. The *injustice* consists in the treatment of those two individuals at the time when they were convicted. An additional, but very much a secondary, cause for concern is the social effect of a miscarriage of justice, if and when discovered, but it is additional and it is secondary. It depends upon the prior recognition that there has been an injustice and does not itself constitute or produce the unjust character of what was done in the past.

Here is another example of the way in which utilitarianism can neglect or distort the role of justice in protesting against wrongs inflicted upon the innocent. This example has nothing to do with punishment. It illustrates how utility and justice can conflict outside the processes of law. Ancient Greek myth includes a tale of the sacrifice of Iphigeneia by her father Agamemnon, leader of the Greek expedition against Troy. The Greek fleet could not set sail because a great storm raged for an inordinately long time. Agamemnon was advised by his soothsayer that the goddess who had raised the storm would be appeased only by the sacrifice of Iphigeneia. Agamemnon reluctantly agreed, Iphigeneia was killed, the storm died down, and the fleet set sail. Agamemnon agreed because he thought that the public good required it. He followed the claim of social utility. The point which I wish to make is not simply that twentieth-century Europeans would call his action incredibly wicked. It is that most ancient Greeks would have done so. The horror of his action imprinted itself upon the Greek consciousness because it was the sacrifice of an innocent person, and his own child to boot.

You might want to say that the sacrifice could not be justified in utilitarian terms because Agamemnon and his companions were mistaken in their superstitious belief that storms can be abated by human sacrifice; the action was not really useful. But this defence of utilitarianism will not do. It is no good saying that the utilitarian criterion of right action is actual rather than supposed utility. When a person has to decide what is the right thing for him to do and takes account of useful and harmful consequences, he can only go on his opinion of what the consequences are likely to be. He can consult others whom he thinks trustworthy, just as Agamemnon consulted his soothsayer, but he cannot command the kind of knowledge which might be available to later generations. He must act on the opinion available at the time. The criterion of utility is itself quite useless if it says that the right action is the one which in fact would be the most useful. To be a genuine criterion for use, it must say that the right action, or at least the action which a person ought to do, is the one which (after informing himself as best he can) he thinks is likely to be the most useful. Agamemnon did what he thought was most useful, after taking the best advice available to him. According to utilitarianism, Agamemnon did what was right.

A utilitarian may say that my examples misunderstand the theory. The *general rule* (no killing or harming of persons who are innocent of any wrong) is almost always useful. The police in my hypothetical example of a cover-up are well aware of this rule. Even in the days of Agamemnon everyone accepted the rule that it is wrong to kill the innocent (and especially your own close kin), so that Agamemnon should have known he was doing wrong. The reason why it is wrong is that it is almost always contrary to utility. The exceptional case does not warrant breaking the rule, if only because breaking the rule will be harmful as an example. If the police allow the conviction of Paddy O'Connor, they will be tempted to bend the law on other occasions and so will gradually impair respect for the generally useful rule than only the guilty should be punished. If Agamemnon sacrifices his innocent daughter, others will say that what is right for Agamemnon is right for them, and again a generally useful rule will cease to command respect. By this line of argument some utilitarians have tried to defend a version of utilitarianism ('rule-utilitarianism') which outdoes intuitionism in its worship of the sacrosanct character of ordinary moral rules.

The defence is futile for a genuine utilitarianism. The whole point of saying that an instance is exceptional is that here it is useful to *break* the rule. Even intuitionists agree that a moral rule must at times be broken, when it conflicts with another which appears paramount in the circumstances. The utilitarian says the reason why the first rule should be broken is that it is more useful to do so. If an agent genuinely thinks that it would be more useful to break a rule in exceptional circumstances (i.e. in circumstances which do not conform to the general pattern in which following the rule is most useful), acceptance of the principle of utility as the overriding criterion requires that he ought to break the rule. The rule that it is right to keep promises is generally useful but not always. No sensible utilitarian would say that one ought to keep a promise in *all* circumstances. Breaking a promise in the exceptional case where some other consideration is clearly more important (the utilitarian would say clearly more useful) does not have the effect of impairing respect for promise-keeping as a general rule. The exceptional case justifies departure from the rule precisely because it is exceptional, different from the general run of cases. And if all moral rules depend on utility, what is true for the rule of promise-keeping is equally true for the rule of not harming the innocent. Generally this is useful. In the exceptional case, like that of Paddy O'Connor or of Iphigeneia, it appears to the agent concerned (the police in the one instance, Agamemnon in the other) that it would be more useful to break the rule. Useful – but immoral. So utility cannot be the sole criterion of morality.

(iv) The story of Agamemnon and Iphigeneia illustrates yet another objection to utilitarianism. Agamemnon's sacrifice of Iphigeneia is especially horrible (and was so to the ancient Greeks) because it was not only the slaughter of an innocent but also the killing by a father of his own child. Utilitarianism neglects the often highly personal character of moral obligation, the fact that it depends on special personal relationship. The point is brought out admirably, if perversely, by an eighteenth-century utilitarian, William Godwin. Suppose, said Godwin (*Political Justice*, II.ii; and *Thoughts on Dr Parr's Spital Sermon*), the palace of Archbishop Fénelon is on fire and you have the time to rescue only one of the two people trapped inside, the Archbishop and his chambermaid, who also happens to be your mother. Fénelon is well known to be a gifted prelate and writer, highly useful to his fellow-men. The chambermaid is a person of limited ability, who will not be missed except by her immediate family, including yourself, her son. Which of the two should you rescue? Natural inclination, Godwin agreed, will lead you to give the preference to your mother, and no doubt almost anyone faced with that choice would in fact rescue his mother and not Fénelon. But, Godwin continued, the *right* action would be to rescue Fénelon instead, because that would bring more benefit to mankind. Godwin knew very well that his conclusion would seem outrageous, for in subsequent editions of his book he tried to make his view less unpalatable by dropping the original character of chambermaid/mother and replacing it with valet/father or brother. He hoped that if misplaced ideas of chivalry were removed, the rationality of his utilitarian judgement would become more apparent. Needless to say, his critics still thought his recommendation was mad.

The examples of Agamemnon and of Godwin's rescuer illustrate the special force in morality of a personal connection such as close kinship. The same thing applies to the personal connection between friends. A utilitarian will say that the reason why we normally have a stronger obligation to our relations and friends than to strangers is social utility. The solidarity of families and of groups of friends produces happiness throughout society with a maximum of efficiency. The feeling of loyalty to family and friends affects only a small circle, but within that circle it gives strong support; and if practically everyone belongs to at least one such circle, then practically everyone is benefited to a marked degree. By contrast, if most people aimed directly at benefiting the whole of society, their efforts would be dissipated and the resulting bits of benefit to any one individual would not add up to a substantial total.

If this were the true foundation of obligations of special relationship, then Godwin would be right in urging us to cast off the natural ties of loyalty to family and friends in circumstances where it is clear that we can thereby contribute more to social utility. After all, there are times when a normal moral consciousness would agree that personal ties must give way to direct public service (e.g. if our country is at war for what we judge to be good and sufficient reasons) – but not to the extent of actually killing one's own child, as Agamemnon did, or of deliberately choosing to rescue a stranger rather than one's own parent, as Godwin recommended. The personal ties count for more than elements in social utility.

Even in the absence of ties binding particular persons together in a special moral relationship, the personal character of human life has a central importance for morality which is neglected by utilitarianism. The point can be brought out in the following way.

According to utilitarianism, the aim of morality is a maximum total amount of happiness for a maximum number of people. Then it follows that we ought to increase world population as far as possible so long as this will not increase unhappiness rather than happiness. The consideration that a world population of 12,000,000,000 people would, *on average*, have a less happy life than a population of 6,000,000,000 (or that a British population of 100,000,000 would, on average, have a less happy life than a population of 50,000,000) is not the decisive factor. If the average happiness of an individual in the larger (doubled) population is 51 per cent of the average happiness of an individual in the smaller population, then the *total amount* of happiness in the former case will be substantially greater than in the latter, and of course that larger total of happiness will also be spread over twice as many people. So, according to utilitarianism, it is clearly a duty to oppose contraception and to urge one's fellow-men to 'be fruitful and multiply'. This is obviously contrary to the moral sentiments of advanced civilizations.

The trouble is that utilitarianism thinks simply of the amount of pleasure or happiness in the abstract, instead of thinking about the *persons* who will be made happy or unhappy. If one said that the aim of morality is to make persons happy, it would not follow that increasing the number of persons should take precedence over the quality of life of existing persons.

This criticism, that utilitarianism is mistaken in fastening upon the amount of happiness as such, needs to be distinguished from a criticism often made, namely that the utilitarian idea of calculating amounts of happiness is impracticable. That particular criticism is misconceived. It is true that no precise calculation can be made of the amount of happiness or unhappiness which alternative actions are likely to produce. But often one can make a rough estimate. More important, one *has* to make it. Any tolerable theory of the standard or standards of right action must include, as an element, the probable consequences of action in terms of happiness and unhappiness, and so it has to reckon with the difficulty of estimating those consequences. The difficulty is a practical one of real life. It is not a theoretical difficulty which comes up for one theory but not for another. We can and we do, indeed we must, estimate roughly that we are likely to produce more happiness or more unhappiness by acting in this way rather than that. Utilitarianism is in no worse plight than any other tolerable theory in facing the fact that such estimation is rough and ready.

Where utilitarianism goes wrong is in fastening upon the estimation of amount of happiness as such, instead of viewing the concept of happiness as subordinate to that of a person. Happiness is important for ethics because it is the chief aim of persons.

6 Kantian ethics

For all its initial attractions, utilitarianism will not do as a theory of the standard of morals. Intuitionism, however, is not satisfactory either. It gives a reasonably accurate picture of everyday moral judgement but it does not meet the needs of a philosophical theory, which should try to show connections and tie things up in a coherent system. To look for unity where none exists would, of course, be foolish; if the diversity of moral rules were intractable, it would be pointless to go on searching for some way of tying them up together. But the moral rules of ordinary life are not obviously all different from each other. As we have seen, intuitionists disagree about the connection or lack of connection between them; and certain of the rules (e.g. promoting happiness and avoiding unhappiness for other people) undoubtedly have a close connection with each other. Is there a theory which can be more successful than utilitarianism in unifying the moral rules of everyday life and of intuitionism? I think there is a principle which is more satisfactory than the utilitarian principle in suggesting a single foundation for all moral rules, though it does not provide a standard for decision when there is a conflict between rules.

This principle was stated by Kant, who distinguished the Categorical (moral) Imperative from Hypothetical (prudential or technical) Imperatives. A hypothetical imperative has the form: 'Do *X* if . . .' or 'You ought to do *X* if . . .'. For example: 'If you want to be healthy, take plenty of exercise'; 'if you want a level surface, use a plane'. The categorical imperative does not depend on an 'if'; the action prescribed is not simply a means to an end. For instance, the moral injunction 'Be kind to others' does not mean 'Be kind to others if you want to avoid making enemies of them'; kindness is prescribed for its own sake and not for the sake of some further (self-interested) end.

Kant gave three formulations of the categorical imperative, i.e. of the fundamental principle of moral action. (Sometimes he wrote as if there were four formulations, but two of these were variations on a single theme and I think that a threefold formula shows more clearly the different aspects of his theory.) The first concerns the *form* of the categorical imperative; the second concerns its *content*; and the third links these together.

(1) Act as if you were legislating for everyone.
(2) Act so as to treat human beings always as ends and never merely as means.
(3) Act as if you were a member of a realm of ends.

The first of these prescriptions is a method of avoiding partiality. It says that when you are considering whether an action is morally right or wrong, you should ask yourself whether you would want everyone to act in that way. In other words, it is not moral to make exceptions for yourself. This formula does not tell us what makes an action right; it simply gives us one way of seeing whether an action would be wrong – by considering what would happen if everyone acted like that. Kant sometimes put the idea in a slightly different form: act as if you were laying down a universal law of nature. This is virtually telling you to imagine that your decision was one taken by God, affecting everyone. You should treat your decision as if it were a law for everyone to follow.

I have said that (1) concerns the *form* of the categorical imperative because it shows that a moral judgement, employing the word 'ought' in a moral sense, has the form of a universal prescription. 'I ought' – or 'You ought' – 'morally to do *X*' does not simply have the character of a straightforward exhortation or command addressed to one person: 'Let me do *X*' – or 'Do *X*'. It implies that anyone and everyone in this sort of situation is equally required to do *X*.

Formulation (2) concerns *content* and therefore supplies the standard of morally right action. 'Act so as to treat human beings always as ends and never merely as means.' This needs explanation.

We constantly treat people as means. If I ask a skilled carpenter to make and put up bookshelves for me, or if I ask a restaurant-owner to produce a meal for me, I use each of them as a means to my ends or purposes; just as I can use instruments such as a saw and a drill as a means to making and putting up the bookshelves myself, or saucepans and a cooker to produce the meal myself. When my College employs me to teach philosophy, it uses me as a means to its end or purpose of broadening the education of its students.

There is nothing wrong with treating a person as a means so long as you do not treat him *merely* as a means. A slave is treated merely as a means. A slave, said Aristotle, is a living tool. When I use a carpenter or a restaurateur as I might use an instrument, I do not treat him merely as a means. I ask him what is his charge and I agree to pay the charge. When my College offers me a post as a teacher, it offers me a salary. There is a transaction into which each party enters freely. The carpenter wants jobs, the restaurateur wants customers; they want to exercise their skills and to earn money. When I ask the carpenter to make and put up the bookshelves, the work serves his purposes as well as mine. In asking him to do the job and in agreeing to his price for it, I have regard to his ends as well as my own.

To treat a person 'as an end' is to act on the recognition that he has purposes just as you have. These purposes can be divided into two classes: (*a*) desires, (*b*) choices. To treat a man as an end, said Kant, is to make his ends your own, i.e. to act towards his purposes as you naturally do towards your own; it is to act so as to help secure those purposes. If I employ a man and pay him an agreed wage, I act so as to help satisfy his desires as well as my own. If (unlike a slave-owner in relation to a slave) I respect his choices, i.e. if I either help him to carry them out or leave him free to fulfil them himself, then I treat him as an end; I regard his choices, like my own, as things to be implemented. To treat a person as an end, then, is to help fulfil his desires and to allow or enable him to carry out his decisions. If you treat a person always as an end, there is nothing wrong with treating him at the same time as a means. What would be wrong is to treat him *merely* as a means to your own ends. It follows from this that the attribute of being morally wrong applies not only to enslavement but also to domination (which makes no allowance for the dominated person's power of deciding for himself) and to the failure to help people who need your help and whom you could help.

Formulation (3) connects (1) and (2) together. It tells you to act as 'a member of a realm of ends'. 'Realm' here means a State, a politically organized society. The idea is that you should act as a member of a community of persons, *all* of whom make moral decisions. This implies that each member treats all the others as moral beings; he has regard to their desires, allows them freedom of decision, *and* recognizes that everyone can and should decide as if legislating for all. You must accept that other people are just as competent as yourself to make universally legislative decisions. This joins the universality of moral decision to the fact that moral action treats people as ends. It implies a form of *equality* for all men; it requires us to recognize that every human being equally has the power to make choices and decisions, including moral decisions of what would be right for everyone.

It will be seen that the Kantian theory of ethics, like the utilitarian, has political implications. Kantian ethics is in fact an ethics of democracy. It requires liberty (allow everyone to decide for himself), equality (in the sense explained a moment ago), and fraternity (think of yourself as a member of a moral community).

The utilitarian principle – or rather, the aim that utilitarianism was really after – can be derived from the second formulation of Kantian ethics as a consequence of it. If you treat every person as an end, you must have regard to his desires (a major sector of his ends) and you must, when you can, help him to fulfil his desires. Since everyone desires happiness for himself and freedom from unhappiness, to treat all human beings as ends requires the promotion of their happiness and the prevention or diminution of their unhappiness.

One qualification, however, must be made to this statement that Kantian ethics implies the gist of utilitarianism as a consequence. The utilitarians included the pleasure and pain of all sentient creatures in their theory. Kant's formulation, on the other hand, is confined to the treatment of human beings and says nothing about the treatment of other animals. This is mainly because Kant emphasized the place of rationality in ethics. To regard someone as an end is to respect (a) his desires, (b) his power of decision. The second of these applies only to rational beings, and so (if we assume that non-human animals do not have enough rational capacity to take decisions) it is not possible to regard an animal fully as an end. Kant may also have been influenced by the fact that most people do not think it immoral to use animals merely as means when they are killed for food. Since Kant's formulations of the categorical imperative are intended to bring to light the principles which underlie normal moral consciousness, it seems to follow that the principle of treating other beings as ends and not merely as means does not extend to the treatment of non-human animals. Nevertheless, as an account of normal moral consciousness, Kant's presentation must be defective, since we do think it morally wrong to cause pain to animals unless as a necessary evil for the sake of a more important moral end; and quite a lot of people have doubts about the *ethics* of killing animals for food even if they do not act on their doubts. So I think that Kant's second principle, the one which gives the content of the categorical imperative, should be extended to read: 'Act so as to treat rational and/or sensitive beings as ends and not merely as means.' This will imply having a regard for the desires of animals and so not causing them pain unless for a more important moral end. It still allows us to say that human beings are more important than other animals because the other animals count as ends in a more limited sense. Whether or not this justifies the killing of animals for food is a question on which disagreement will remain.

The Kantian principle has some affinity with the Golden Rule of biblical (and other) ethics, 'Do unto others as you would they should do unto you'; but it is even closer to the precept of the Old Testament which St. Matthew's Gospel finds equivalent to the Golden Rule, 'Act lovingly towards your neighbour, for he is like yourself'.[1] Treating others as ends means acting towards their purposes (desires and choices) as you would act naturally towards your own; it means trying to give effect to those purposes. The Golden Rule is commonly taken to be the foundation of the whole of ethics, and the same thing can be said of the principle of treating rational and sentient beings as ends. The mere fact that utilitarian ethics can be derived from Kantian (when the latter is modified to include animals) shows that the principle of ends does at least as well as the principle of utility in providing such a foundation. Whether it does any better we can judge by looking again at the questions which raised difficulties for utilitarianism.

(i) Self-evidence. How do we reach the principle of ends? Is it supposed to be self-evident? Kant himself was a rationalist. He maintained that the categorical imperative is known to be true by the exercise of reason. We do not have to follow him in that view. If, on general philosophical grounds, we think it is best to follow the path of empiricism, i.e. to explain ideas and beliefs in terms of the experience of sense and feeling, then we can explain our fundamental ethical principle in this sort of way, just as an empiricist utilitarian does with his principle. The capacity for imaginative sympathy is what enables us to judge and act as moral beings. We can imagine ourselves in other people's shoes; we can imagine what we should want and how we should decide if we were in their situation. Sympathy is what leads us to act so as to serve other people's ends, to feel towards their ends as we naturally feel towards our own. Quite apart from the general philosophical grounds for preferring empiricism to rationalism, an advantage of this view over Kant's position is that it explains why we have moral obligations to non-human as well as to human animals.

This empiricist approach to the principle of ends does not give a complete answer to the question, how do we know the truth of our fundamental principle. As with the empiricist form of utilitarianism, it does not show how we are to proceed from positive psychological explanation to normative judgement. The account tells us that sympathy produces a judgement and a motive of altruistic obligation to be set alongside the innate motive of self-interest. But it has not explained why

---

[1] I follow the view of Edward Ullendorff that the correct translation of Lev. 19:18 is something like this and not, as in the Authorized Version, 'Thou shalt love thy neighbour as thyself'. See his convincing essay, 'Thought Categories in the Hebrew Bible', in Raphael Loewe (ed.), *Studies in Rationalism, Judaism and Universalism: in Memory of Leon Roth* (1966), especially pp.276–8.

Matt.7:12 says that the Golden Rule 'is the law and the prophets'; Matt.22:40 says that the commandments to love God and one's neighbour are the two on which 'hang all the law and the prophets'.

the claims of sympathy should be regarded as superior to those of self-interest. The empiricist version of utilitarianism was similarly defective, though it wanted to reach the different normative judgement that the claims of self and of others should be ranked equally.

As regards the first objection to utilitarianism, then, the principle of ends fares no better and no worse. The rationalist version of either theory says that its fundamental principle is self-evident, but the alleged self-evidence is something of a mystery and is not accepted by everyone. The empiricist version gives a positive psychological explanation of the feeling of obligation to others but fails to give us a good reason for making a normative judgement about altruistic obligation in relation to natural self-interest.

(ii) Resolution of conflict. Utilitarianism provides no criterion for resolving conflicts between its two principles of aggregation and of distribution. The principle of ends does not consist of two elements which can conflict with each other, but it still has trouble about conflicts because the single prescription to treat rational and sensitive beings as ends is not an aggregative principle requiring the greatest possible degree of something. One is often faced with a situation where the claims of different people to be treated as ends cannot all be met. If I help Peter I shall fail to help Paul, yet I ought to treat them both as ends.

This does not mean that the principle of ends makes the impossible demand that I should be helping everyone at all times. As Kant pointed out, to say that someone *ought* to do something is to imply that he *can* do it. A man's moral obligations cannot exceed his capacity. Utilitarianism takes account of this when it says that your duty is to produce as much happiness as you *can* for as many people as you *can*. So the principle of ends does not say that I ought to help both Peter and Paul when it is possible for me to help only one of them. The trouble is that it does not give me a criterion for deciding which of them I should help. It provides a theoretical unity for the different rules of commonsense morality (or of intuitionist theory), just as utilitarianism tries to do, but it does not afford a standard for resolving conflicts. One cannot settle the dilemma of whether to help Peter or Paul by asking 'Shall I satisfy the principle of treating persons as ends more fully if I help Peter or more fully if I help Paul?'

This problem of resolving the conflict between moral claims needs further discussion and I shall come back to it later. Meanwhile we must note that the Kantian principle again does no better than utilitarianism.

(iii) Justice, especially the justice of punishment. The utilitarian view of why we have a penal system at all is obviously sensible. The object of a penal system is utilitarian, the security of society. But when it comes to applying the penal system to accused individuals, two questions need to be asked. The first question is whether punishment is morally *permissible* in this instance. If the answer to that question is yes, then the second question is whether punishment would be *useful* in this instance, and if so, what sort of punishment and how much. Justice comes in by requiring that the answer to the first question be met before the second question may be posed. On the first question, punishment is permissible only if the accused person is guilty: this usually means, only if he has deliberately chosen to break the law, knowing that it was forbidden and that there was a penalty. In these circumstances punishment is morally permissible in two ways. (1) In conversational parlance, when talking about the punishment of an obviously deliberate wrongdoer, we often say he has 'asked for it', meaning that he has deliberately *chosen* it as the consequence of his action if he is caught. Of course his conscious choice was to do the forbidden action rather than to reap the consequence of being caught for doing it, but since he knew the consequence, the punishment does not at any rate go against his choice. To this extent, punishment of a deliberate offender does not fail to treat him as an end. (2) Where an offence does harm to another person, a deliberate offender breaches the principle of treating others as ends. He does not act as a member of a realm of ends and cannot expect to be treated as one. He has put himself outside the moral community, has forfeited his right to be treated as an end. Society is then entitled to treat him *simply* as a means and to do with him what is socially useful. But if an accused person is innocent, punishment is not permitted by the concept of justice, however useful it might be.

Kant himself would have nothing to do with a utilitarian theory of punishment. He followed a throughgoing retributive view; the punishment is called for by the offence and must be inflicted irrespective of good or bad consequences. Most of us would think that such a severe conception borders on the immoral. On the other hand a purely utilitarian theory of punishment, as we have seen, can have immoral implications. The strength of the concept of justice, on the question of punishment, is that it protects the innocent against the encroachments of social utility. Its main role is to set up the first of my two questions: is punishment permissible in this case? Then, if the answer to that question is yes, justice can largely leave it to utility to determine whether in fact any punishment ought to be applied in this instance. The answer to the second question is not entirely a matter for utility, however. It might sometimes be useful to sentence an offender to an 'exemplary' punishment, that is, one more severe than the particular offence really warrants. If so, the punishment goes beyond what is just, what the offender deserves. In such circumstances a judge ought to balance the claim of social utility against that of justice. It is worth noting that in this respect, too, the idea that punishment is a matter of just deserts serves to protect the individual, even if not innocent, against the demands of social utility.

Where utilitarianism failed to take account of the powerful plea of justice on behalf of the individual, the principle of ends makes clear what is involved. A deliberate offender has forfeited his right to be treated as an end. To the extent that he has done so (but, as a matter of justice, no further than that), he may be treated as a means to the ends of society without regard to his own ends (his wishes). But even this, in a sense, is not going against his ends (his choices) because he deliberately chose a course of action which he knew was liable to lead to punishment.

(iv) The personal character of morality. The principle of ends does not surmount the whole of the objection to utilitarianism on the score of special personal relationships. In telling us to treat all human beings as ends (in the full sense of respecting both desires and choices), it does not show why moral obligation to relations and friends is stronger than to other people. To be sure, it would not run directly counter to ordinary moral consciousness by requiring that you should rescue Archbishop Fénelon in preference to your mother on the ground that he will be more useful to society. To this extent it is less objectionable than utilitarianism. Godwin's view asks you to think of Fénelon and his servant simply as means. If you follow the Kantian precept and think of them as ends, they both have a claim to be rescued, and you are not entitled to prefer Fénelon on grounds of utility. Thus far the principle of ends is sounder than utilitarianism. But it does not explain why you should give preference to your mother. The hypothetical situation is an example of a conflict of claims, and we have already seen that the principle of ends fails to provide a criterion for settling such conflicts.

It does, however, take account of the personal character of morality as regards the effects of action. On the Kantian view, the right action is not a matter of producing a maximum of happiness as such. Kant's principle requires us to treat persons as ends. So if we are faced with a choice between improving (or maintaining) the quality of life for existing persons and increasing the number of persons at the expense of average happiness, the Kantian principle leads us to prefer the former alternative, because we have to take account of the wishes and choices of existing persons, while on the other side future potential persons are mere possibilities. Of course it is conceivable that most of the people who now exist might themselves choose to sacrifice part of their own happiness in order to have a larger population. In that event, having regard to their ends would require preference for the second alternative.

The point is that the principle of ends does not imply, as utilitarianism does, a conclusion which is contrary to the actual moral consciousness of our time.

The upshot of this survey is that the principle of ends does better than utilitarianism in meeting the claims of justice and (partially) in account-ing for the personal character of ethics. Both theories leave a gap in explaining how we arrive at an ethical outlook, and both fail to supply a single criterion for settling a conflict of claims.

Intuitionism is certainly no more satisfactory than the principle of ends in dealing with the difficulties that remain. For example, it says that self-evident principles of ethics are known by intuition and that a conflict between principles is to be resolved by intuition. But the same word here is used in two different senses. The 'intuiting' of a self-evident principle is supposed to be an intellectual grasp of a necessary truth, while the 'intuiting' of the resolution of a conflict between principles is supposed to be the result of weighing up the different strengths or stringencies of the conflicting obligations or claims. The former is compared with the use of the intellect in a formal science like logic or mathematics, when we understand the necessary connection between the subject and predicate of an axiom or between the premisses and conclusion of an inference; the latter is compared with the exercise of judgement in empirical science, when we weigh the evidence for and against a hypothesis. The one kind of 'intuition' leads to necessity, the other to probability.

It can be said once again that intuitionism is inadequate as a theory but accurate enough as a picture of commonsense moral thinking. The difference which it portrays, but does not explain, between two kinds of moral judgement calls for some further inquiry. The difference is between a moral judgement which is a straightforward acceptance or application of a general principle and a moral judgement which is the result of deciding between a conflict of principles.

In Chapter 3 I drew attention to a feature of moral judgement which has been especially emphasized by Professor R.M. Hare, its universality, and I said that in this matter Hare was reviving an aspect of Kant's theory. In the present chapter we have seen how Kant brought out this universality in his first formulation of the categorical imperative. Kant compares moral judgement with legislation; we should think of our moral judgements as if we were laying down a law for everyone to follow. This analogy seems helpful and sound when applied to the enunciation of a moral rule or to the simple application of a rule to a particular instance: 'I ought to keep promises' or 'I must be at Piccadilly Circus by 12 noon because I have promised to meet my friend John there at that time.' The obligation is not peculiar to me. Everyone ought to keep promises;

anyone who has promised to meet a friend at a definite time and place has an obligation to be in that place at that time. But is it so clear that the moral judgement which resolves a conflict, a dilemma, should be regarded as universally applicable, as legislating for everyone?

We need to take a serious example of a moral dilemma in order to see the point. In a case of conflict where almost everyone would agree which claim was strongest, there is virtually no real conflict. An example of this is the one I gave in an earlier chapter: someone breaks a promise to meet a friend at the theatre in order to drive to hospital a neighbour who is seriously ill. The moral conclusion may not have a 100 per cent certainty, like the simple obligation to help when there is no conflicting claim, but the one claim so far outweighs the other that it would be silly to say 'I *probably* ought to give preference to helping my neighbour'. It is also useful to take an example from real life instead of a fictitious hypothesis. Jean-Paul Sartre, the French twentieth-century existentialist, brought out the point well when he discussed the dilemma of a young friend of his in occupied France during the Second World War. The young man was faced with the choice of going off to join the Resistance Movement or staying with his widowed mother. (The example makes much more sense than Godwin's fictitious example of whether to rescue Archbishop Fénelon or one's mother.) Which alternative ought he to prefer? There is no obvious answer to the question. If the young man decides that he ought to join the Resistance, will he also think that this would be the proper decision for anyone else in his situation? On the contrary, since he has found the decision such a difficult one, will he not judge that someone else who decides the other way is just as much entitled to his decision? In a genuine moral dilemma, there is no answer which tells us what is *the* right thing to do. There is a good deal to be said for each of the alternatives. It is up to the individual to decide, and when a particular individual does decide, he knows that someone else might decide differently and he does not think that his own decision is the one which others ought necessarily to follow.

If the straightforward kind of moral judgement can be compared with legislation, the resolution of a moral dilemma is better compared with one kind of adjudication, the decision by a court of law that one claim overrides another. Legislation is an Act of Parliament, a general statement that such and such action is required of everyone in certain specified circumstances. This is like the formulation of a general moral principle. Adjudication by a court is sometimes a matter of determining whether a particular situation is or is not covered by a legal rule, and that is like deciding whether a moral principle applies to an individual circumstance (e.g. whether a 'white lie' is a lie, properly speaking, and so is to be condemned as wrong). At other times adjudication by a court is a matter of deciding which of two conflicting claims or rules should be regarded as paramount, and this is like deciding what to do in a moral dilemma. A conflict of legal claims which provides no real difficulty (like the easily settled moral conflict between the claim of the sick neighbour to be driven to hospital and the claim of the friend to be met at the theatre) does not normally come into court; it is settled 'out of court' on the advice of solicitors. The cases which come to court are those in which it is perfectly possible for an experienced judge to prefer either of the alternative decisions available, and indeed if the case goes as far as an appeal hearing before more than one judge, the judges are frequently divided in their conclusions. In law, the decision which is finally reached by a higher court, even if reached by only a majority of one, is, to be sure, regarded as a binding precedent for future cases. This means that adjudication in such cases has the force of legislation; in the next case raising the same issues, there will be no dilemma. But that is done as a matter of convenience, to save further expense and uncertainty. The same considerations do not apply to the dilemmas of ethics. On the contrary, there are sound reasons for saying that in ethics we should *not* simply follow the example of someone else but should try to make up our own minds, to act as moral beings capable of taking decisions on difficult problems of human life.

That is the centre of gravity in Sartre's existentialist ethics. The most important thing about the human condition, in Sartre's view, is that we can choose for ourselves. He concludes that values are the result of choice; we make our values by our choices. If this is applied to all values, it results in a moral anarchy in which a humanistic ethic (like that of Kant or of what we call the 'higher' religions) has no more validity than sadism or fascism or racism. When a racist chooses to give a higher value to one group of human beings than to another, there is, according to this account, no sound reason to criticize his views; values are what any individual makes them. But if the existentialist thesis is applied only to the resolution of a conflict of obligations, it is more sensible, especially since the idea of universality seems out of place for such decisions.

Even this restricted use of Sartre's view needs some further qualification. Sartre talked as if the choice which made a man's values were entirely irrational or non-rational. We just 'choose', out of the blue. 'Freedom has struck me, like a thunderbolt', says Orestes in Sartre's play *Les Mouches*. But that is not *choice*. Sartre's young friend in real life, when faced with his dilemma, had to *think* about his conflicting obligations, and had to *decide* in the end that one of them was more important or had the greater claim upon him or something of the kind.

In discussing the first, epistemological difficulty posed for Kantian ethics, as for intuitionism and utilitarianism, I said that we need not follow Kant in treating the principle of ends as a self-evident truth. We can explain it as having arisen from imaginative sympathy. Imaginative sympathy produces a *feeling* of obligation, a motive for acting so as to help meet the ends of the person with whom we sympathize. It is strongest towards those with whom we are in close association. That is why the ties of friendship and family relationship are felt with especial strength. When we *think* about the knowledge of other persons which is given to us by imaginative sympathy, we realize that all human beings are in the same boat, having desires and choices and lacking self-sufficiency. We thus reach the Kantian principle of regarding all human beings as ends. Further reflection leads to the revised principle of ends which has regard also to non-human animals. Intellectually, then, we can see that the principle of ends extends to all rational and sensitive beings. But the strength of our *feelings* depends on our personal associations. One man may feel that his obligation to his widowed mother is stronger than his obligation to all who are oppressed by the Nazis. Another man may be so affected by imaginative building upon some experience relating to the plight of the larger group that he feels a stronger obligation to them.

This is a suggested psychological *explanation* of the way in which people *do* decide between a conflict of claims and why different individuals decide differently. (It also sketches an explanation of why ties of special personal relationship count for so much in ethics, a point which was not covered by a simple reading of the principle of ends.) It does not propose a *criterion* of how we *should* decide. I do not think it is possible to provide that; there is no one right answer for the resolution of a moral dilemma. But at least the explanation shows that the decision is not just a blind leap in the dark. It depends upon the moral factors of imagination and sympathetic feeling.

Ethics and politics

7 Justice

At first sight, politics seems quite opposed to the spirit of ethics. The keynote of ethics is altruism, while politics is more hard-boiled; politics has to reckon with the predominance of self-interest in human nature and exemplifies this in the behaviour of politicians themselves as they jockey for power. All the same, most politicians think of their objectives in ethical terms – the public interest, social justice, freedom from oppression or freedom from want. The relative emphasis which a political party gives to some of these ideas defines its political stance, even though its actions are often motivated by less high-flown sentiments. Conservatives and liberals emphasize freedom and individual initiative, socialists emphasize equality and social justice.

Differences of political attitude and ideology crystallize especially around the two concepts of justice and liberty. Everybody is in favour of justice, but not the same interpretation of it. Everybody is in favour of freedom or liberty, but not the same kind of freedom. Left-wingers give priority to 'social justice' with an intention to reform society in the direction of greater equality and the removal of poverty. A right-winger's concept of justice (he is unlikely to use the phrase 'social justice') sets more store by the virtues of law and order, of stability, of reward for enterprise and merit. Right-wingers also stress freedom and connect this with enterprise, with minimal interference by the State, with encouraging people to stand on their own feet. Left-wingers attach less importance to these things as compared with the necessity of State intervention, with social solidarity, indeed with 'social justice'. This does not mean that the left-winger attaches no importance to liberty. On the contrary, he agrees that it is a fundamental value and wants to retain it as a social goal so long as it does not get out of hand, especially in the economic life of the community. Or rather, this is true of a left-winger who is also a democrat. People who do not believe in democracy (and they may be either on the left or on the right of the political spectrum) are different. They have little regard for liberty as ordinarily understood; they advocate instead a peculiar interpretation of liberty and use it as a defence-mechanism when they are charged with sacrificing the individual to the collective interest of the State.

Justice and liberty are the two most basic ideas of all political thought. Every society needs some sort of structure to be maintained, and every *reflective* society needs some sort of *concept* concerning that structure. Justice is the basic concept of social value; it is what holds a society together. But since every society consists of individual persons, there is bound to be a tension between social cohesion and the feelings of independence and separate identity experienced by every individual human being. This is given expression in the concept of liberty. Justice and liberty are therefore liable to be contrasted with each other: justice is a social virtue, while liberty is very much concerned with the individual, ready among other things to defend the rights of the individual against the demands of the State. Justice, however, has more than one facet, and it often goes along with liberty in standing up for the individual against the claims of society as a whole. We saw this in Chapters 5 and 6; a utilitarian concern for the general welfare of society can come into conflict with ideas of justice for the individual.

Justice is a complex concept. It appears both in law and in ethics, and in each of these spheres of thought it has a conservative aspect and a reformative aspect. The whole of law is said to be concerned with justice. Judges are appointed to do justice according to law. Whether they are administering criminal or civil law, their function is to serve the interests of justice. In ethics the concept of justice is less pervasive. Justice is one of the virtues, not a comprehensive name for all of them. It is the most basic of the social virtues and so is in a way the most important of them. But from another point of view it can be called less important, or at least less admirable, than virtues which go beyond it in not being expected as a matter of course: virtues like generosity, bravery, self-sacrifice. Justice in law and justice in ethics are distinct but not separate concepts. The idea of justice always has an ethical tinge and when it is used in law, or is applied to the legal system as a whole, it is a reminder that law, as commonly understood, is not simply a set of any old rules subject to enforcement; law has an ethical purpose and is normally expected to use ethical methods.

Justice in the law and justice in social ethics, I have said, both have a conservative and a progressive aspect. Let us look first at the law.

Law is predominantly a conservative institution, and lawyers in consequence tend to have a conservative outlook. Law exists to maintain order in society. When lawbreakers are dealt with under the criminal law, the intention is to preserve society and the way it is run. Society has a working structure which depends on following the rules. People who break the rules are made liable to punishment in order to repair the breach, so to speak. When disputes between individuals or groups are considered and settled under the civil law, the intention is to protect an existing system of rights. If one man encroaches on the rights of another, he is liable to be required to restore the balance, by making good the damage or paying compensation or at least undertaking to respect the rights of the injured party in future. The procedures of legal justice, in both these types of instance, are conservative, protecting and restoring an established order.

But the law also has a progressive or reformative aspect. Statutes (laws made by the legislature) change the rules in accordance with new ideas of what is fair and proper. I take some examples from recent legislation in the United Kingdom, but they are typical of recent legislation in many other countries. In the twentieth century there have been new laws about the status and rights of women, enabling them to vote and to stand for election to Parliament, forbidding discrimination against them in opportunities, appointments, and pay. There have been new laws about rights in the family, extending grounds for divorce, changing rules of inheritance. There have been new laws about social security, making the State responsible for meeting basic needs in sickness, old age, and unemployment. There have been new laws about protection at work, requiring safety precautions in factories, forbidding unfair dismissal, limiting the power of employers to make workpeople redundant. There have been new laws about the role of trade unions, recognizing and regulating the right to strike and to seek support for a strike, permitting or forbidding arrangements for a 'closed shop'. The progressive aspect of legal justice comes out most often in statutes, new laws enacted by the legislature. But it can also be seen, though to a lesser extent, in the additions to law which are made by judges. When case law is developed by the decisions of judges, the aim is often simply to clarify what has been uncertain or to remove inconsistency which has arisen inadvertently; but in quite a number of instances the aim goes further than that and modifies or extends the law in the interests of current ethical ideas. A general example is a gradual change in English common law over the past half century, putting persons before property instead of the other way round.[1] A specific example is the famous case of *Donoghue* v. *Stevenson* of 1932 (in fact a Scottish case, but affecting English law also because it was determined by the House of Lords), which was used by senior judges as an opportunity to extend the law of negligence when it was felt to be defective from a moral point of view.[2]

In social ethics, as in law, the conservative aspect of justice upholds the

---

[1] Cf. Lord Denning, giving judgement in the case of *Davis* v *Johnson*, [1979] A.C.264, at 274: 'in the 19th century the law paid quite high regard to rights of property. But ... in modern times the law has changed course. Social justice requires that personal rights should, in a proper case, be given priority over rights of property.'

[2] Cf. Patrick (Lord) Devlin, *The Judge* (1979), p. 94.

established order of things. People are entitled to keep what they have. A man may choose to give away something that belongs to him, but if he wants to hang on to it he has every right to do so. Again, many people feel that it is unjust to upset existing differentials in pay for different jobs; if one group of workers has been overtaken by a group who used to be behind them, they tend to think that justice requires the balance to be restored; they have lost their place in the queue, and queue-jumping is unfair.

At the same time nearly everybody also attributes to justice a reformative role, allowing new rights to be set up on the basis of need or merit. Despite the unfairness of queue-jumping, we do not say 'first come, first served' in all circumstances; if the passengers on a ship in distress have to take to the lifeboats, it is 'women and children first'; if several candidates apply for an appointment, there is no unfairness in preferring the best-qualified to the earliest arrival. The poor and the homeless should be provided for, at the expense of the better off. The supposed justice of retaining differentials for different jobs does not require any class of persons to stay where they are in the established hierarchy; on the contrary, if they are especially talented or especially hard-working, it is just for them to be rewarded and to move up the social scale.

Conservative justice tries to preserve things as they are, on the assumption that everyone benefits from a stable society, despite the defects of any actual social order. Progressive justice tries to remedy the defects, to redistribute rights in such a way as to make a more fair society. But what is fair? There have always been two different, and apparently incompatible, ideas about this.

First there is the idea of justice as depending on merit or desert. It can be seen in criminal justice (an aspect of the conservative role of the concept of justice) as well as in ideas of fairness in social ethics. Criminal justice is a matter of punishing people who are guilty of breaking the law; it would be unjust to punish people who have done nothing to deserve it. Just reward likewise has to do with merit; a reward or a prize should go to the person who has earned it, who deserves it. To pass over the candidate or competitor who deserved the prize and to hand it to somebody who did not deserve it would be unjust, unfair. At the end of a war people who have served the State in the armed forces are given a gratuity in recognition of their service to the community. It would be unfair to treat them no differently from those who have not made the same sort of sacrifice and have been able to continue their normal civilian career. The same sort of thing applies to giving people responsibilities and opportunities. Who should be appointed to a post as manager or foreman, headmaster or teacher? Should it not be the person who is most capable of doing the job? Would it not be unfair to pass over the most meritorious candidate and appoint someone of less merit, less well qualified to do that job? Which student should be awarded first-class honours and a scholarship for postgraduate research? Should it not be the one who has shown high talent in the subject? Would it not be unjust to prefer a less meritorious candidate?

These examples illustrate one idea of justice, in which the determining factor for allotting benefits or burdens is desert. It clearly answers to many of our intuitive convictions. It seems to make a strong case.

But there is another idea of justice, based on equality and need. According to this view, justice requires us to treat all human beings as of equal worth and as having equal claims. It is unjust to discriminate in favour of some and against others – except in order to meet special needs. We should do something special for the poor, the sick, the disabled, because they are disadvantaged as compared with most people. We should try, so far as we can, to bring them up to, or near, equality with the more fortunate. Although discrimination is treating people unequally and so is often unjust (according to an egalitarian concept of justice), discrimination in favour of need has an egalitarian purpose. It gives more to the needy because they have less; it is an attempt to reduce inequality, to approach that ideal of equality for all which would be perfect justice. Other kinds of discrimination, however, are inegalitarian in effect as well as in method; they increase the existing inequalities. The specially talented individual already has an advantage over ordinary people. If you give him special rewards, or special prizes, or a specially good job, you will increase his advantage. It may well be useful to society to do this; the person with special talents for a particular job, such as running a business or running a school, will no doubt bring more benefit to the community in doing that job than would someone else of less talent. So it makes sense to train the talented individual, put him in the responsible job, and pay him well as an incentive. It is socially *useful*, and right for that reason; but do not pretend that it is *just*. Strict justice, according to this view of it, requires us to treat everybody alike, apart from helping underdogs to approach equality with the rest.

That is the second idea of justice, and it too makes a persuasive case. Yet the two ideas of justice are clearly incompatible with each other. How are we to decide between them? Each of them has an intuitive appeal for our moral consciousness, though some people go pretty strongly for the one and some go pretty strongly for the other. Is there any *rational* way of choosing between them?

Professor John Rawls[3] has produced an ingenious suggestion for

[3]*A Theory of Justice* (1971 and 1972).

settling the principles of justice in a rational way. It is intended to be a method of avoiding appeals to intuition with the consequent risk of inconsistent answers. Rawls uses the device of a hypothetical social contract, a notion familiar in earlier political philosophy but employed for a different purpose. Rawls tells us to imagine a number of people who know the general laws of social science but are ignorant of all particular facts, including their own abilities, their own history, their own position in society, or indeed the time and place of that society. They are asked to agree upon principles for the distribution of benefits and burdens. We can suppose, Rawls continues, that they will think about the matter in terms of self-interest, trying to maximize benefits and minimize burdens for themselves. But they do not know where they themselves will be in the scheme of things. They might be at the top of the social scale or they might be at the bottom. So, says Rawls, they will take care to make conditions as good as possible for the person at the bottom of the scale, in case they turn out to be there themselves. Their decisions will be motivated by self-interest but will have the effect of serving the interest of everyone impartially, because of 'the veil of ignorance'. In Rawls's view, that is what constitutes the idea of justice or fairness: it is an institutional arrangement which will benefit everyone impartially, and we can reach an understanding of it by imagining a social contract made in ignorance of one's personal situation.

Rawls is not suggesting that the concept of justice can be identified with an idea of self-interest. Justice is essentially impartial between one person and another. If you ask yourself in any situation what would be the just or fair solution of a problem, you should not think in terms of self-interest, giving yourself priority over others. But the trouble is that if people are simply told to think intuitively in terms of justice, they will come up with different and inconsistent answers. A rational calculation in terms of self-interest will avoid the bare reference to intuitions of justice, but in the ordinary way such a calculation would not give us the impartiality that we need. The hypothesis of making the calculation under a veil of ignorance about one's personal situation is a method of adding impartiality. If I have to provide for my own interests in any and every possible contingency, I am providing for the interests of anyone and everyone, not just for my own.

What, then, is the result of such a hypothetical contract made under a veil of ignorance about particular facts? According to Rawls, people in the imagined situation would go first for a maximum of equal liberty, and then secondly they would agree to such departures from equality as would improve life for everyone, including the least advantaged. The point of the second principle is to make a distinction between just and unjust inequalities. If the giving of special rewards or special opportunities to talented people not only produces substantial benefit for those few, with consequent inequality, but also has the result of improving the general standard of life of the whole community, including the standard of its poorest members, then the inequality is justified. But if benefit accrues only to the privileged group and does nothing to improve the lot of the poor, then it is not justified.

This conclusion gives priority to an equality concept of justice. It also makes some provision for the alternative concept of differential reward, though not in terms of merit, strictly speaking. It says that differential rewards are justified, not because they are deserved by the individuals who get them, but because they benefit the whole community and especially its poorest members. In other words, inequality is supported on the grounds of social utility and of helping the needy. So Rawls's idea of justice maintains priority for the equality/needs concept, including in it a dash of general utility, but really excluding any valuation of merit or desert as such. The conclusion will not be to everyone's taste, but at least it is pretty definite in settling the dilemma of choosing between the two traditional concepts. And if the conclusion really has been reached by a rational process of thought instead of appealing to intuitive conviction, we ought to accept it.

In fact, however, Rawls's conclusions do not rest purely on rational calculations which would seem obvious to anyone. The general idea of equality in the absence of special considerations is rational enough. So is a departure from equality for the sake of benefit for all. But why should there be special emphasis on benefit for the poor? Intuitively, of course, this appeals to our sense of justice, or at any rate to our sense of morality. But does Rawls succeed in showing that it would appeal to our sense of self-interest if we were clothed in a veil of ignorance concerning our personal situation?

Rawls assumes that a rational self-interested man will always play safe, will think most of cushioning his position if he should turn out to be unlucky. Suppose this hypothetical contractor contemplates two alternative forms of society. One follows the policy of a radical Welfare State, always providing quite a soft cushion for the people at the bottom of the social scale but inevitably at the expense of high taxation for the rest, so that nobody is excessively well off. The second society still has a cushion for its poorer members, but a less comfortable cushion, and therefore it can leave scope for a few people to gain glittering prizes as the result of special talent, special effort, or simple luck. If we are asked which of the two is the more *just* society, we may well say the first, but that is an intuitive judgement. If we are asked which of the two would be chosen by a purely *self-interested* individual who did not know what his personal abilities and fortunes would turn out to be, is it clear that he would go for the first alternative? Why should he necessarily play safe and think mainly of what will happen to him if he is unlucky? Why should he not take a bit of a gamble? In the second society, he will not be so badly off even if he lands up at the bottom of the pile, and there is always the chance that he might turn out to be one of the fortunate few.

The idea of self-interest itself does not imply any preference between timidity and boldness in making this choice. Rawls is not justified in assuming that a self-interested man will be timid rather than bold. This is obvious from the fact that Rawls's *first* principle of justice assumes the opposite, namely that a self-interested man will prefer boldness to timidity. The first principle requires a maximum of equal liberty. This means that the people taking part in the hypothetical social contract, and choosing from a self-interested point of view, will give priority to a maximum of liberty for all. Rawls makes it quite clear that his specification of equal liberty, rather than some other kind of equality (equality of material goods, for instance), is deliberate. But is it clear that a self-interested person, abstracting from the kind of society he lives in, would necessarily give the highest priority to freedom? A twentieth-century American like Rawls would do so (as would a twentieth-century Englishman like myself). But what about an ancient Egyptian in the time of Joseph? According to the Old Testament, the Egyptians were prepared to sell themselves into slavery in return for corn. For that matter, what about a twentieth-century citizen of the Soviet Union or of some poverty-stricken country of the Third World? Is it clear that they would give personal freedom a higher priority than economic subsistence? Rawls has not made his veil of ignorance dark enough to blot out all the psychological effects of his own culture. A modern American sets a high value on personal liberty; he wants to be free to do his own thing, and he has enough confidence in his own powers to be bold in accepting the risks of freedom. In other cultures, present and past, harsh conditions have induced most people to be more fearful and to regard limitations on personal freedom as inevitable if one is to stay alive. Assuming that it makes sense at all to think of self-interested persons making choices in genuine ignorance of their own situation and un-affected by the experience of a particular society, why should we say that their choice would be bold rather than timid in selecting their first principle of justice, and timid rather than bold in selecting their second principle?

Rawls's device of a social contract, then, does not give us a rational method of deciding between the two rival concepts of justice. The purpose of the device is to reach impartiality. But that can be done in a simpler way. To get away from a self-interested to an impartial judgement, all you need do is to imagine yourself in the shoes of someone else. You can exercise that capacity for imaginative sympathy which I described in Chapter 6. Is not this in fact the psychological basis of the needs concept of justice? If one says that justice requires special attention to the needs of the poor, the idea of self-interest is quite irrelevant. It is not a question of making sure that there will be help for yourself if you ever find yourself landed among the poor (as indeed you might). It is a question of forgetting about yourself for the moment and thinking of people who *are* poor. It does involve a kind of self-identification with the poor, because you can only appreciate what they feel if you imagine what you would feel if you were one of them. But that is not supposing that you really are one of them, and the moral judgement which it produces is an altruistic one, not a self-interested insurance policy.

The question that does need to be raised is whether the moral obligation which arises from sympathy for the disadvantaged is an obligation of *justice*. People who favour the merit concept of justice will not deny that there is a moral obligation to help the needy, but they will deny that it is an obligation of justice. It is the duty of charity, they will say, a finer thing than justice but not to be confused with it. Justice has to do with entitlements or rights. There is no right to charity, as there is a right to what you have earned for yourself. Charity is a matter of grace and favour. To be sure, a conscientious person will feel that he has a duty to be charitable; if he thinks of himself merely as doing a favour, he tarnishes the brightness of charity as a virtue. But for the recipient it is a favour, not a right. As a duty charity is a 'duty of supererogation', it goes beyond what is absolutely required of us by duties of 'perfect obligation', by the demands of justice.

From the other side, one can retort that the merit concept of justice is equally misguided in attributing to justice an idea which belongs to a different part of ethics. It is morally appropriate to reward merit, but does the meritorious person have a right to that reward? If he were to claim it as his right, he would tarnish the brightness of the merit which we attribute to him. This is true even of reward for a rendered service, but how much more true is it of award for talent. If a prize or a scholarship or a responsible job is awarded to the most meritorious candidate, the one with the greatest talent for the subject of competition, it is proper to say that he merits the award but hardly that he has a right to it. Sometimes it is reasonable enough to think of the winner as having a right; if a competition has been publicized in terms that amount to a contract with those who take part, then the winner has a contractual right to the prize which has been promised to the most successful competitor. But the most talented candidate for a scholarship or an appointment does not have a right to it, although it is right that he should get it. Well, why is it right? A critic of the merit concept of justice may say it is right because it is useful. Merit, whether it takes the form of service conferred or of talent exhibited, is praised because it is socially useful. It is rewarded because the reward is itself useful, an incentive to the meritorious individual to continue to practise his useful activity, and an incentive to others to emulate him if they can. Social utility does not cover the whole field of the morally right, as the utilitarians claimed, but it is undoubtedly a major, indeed the major, part of the morally right. So there is certainly a moral duty to reward merit, a duty based on utility. But utility is not justice; utility often comes into conflict with justice. The rightness of rewarding merit is not a requirement of justice.

Criticism and counter-criticism here both go too far. There is, in the Western world at least, a strong tradition which makes justice embrace some degree of charity. It is also a long tradition. Although prominent in socialist theory of the nineteenth century, it goes back to the Bible (both Old and New Testaments) and as a result finds legal expression in medieval canon law. There are two reasons for the tendency to turn charity into justice.

The first is effective coverage. If help for the needy is left to private initiative, it is apt to be spasmodic in its effects. When it is made a matter of justice, this means that it becomes a responsibility of the community as a whole, something to be included in a mandatory system of tithes or taxes, so that everyone who can afford to contribute is required to do so, and everyone who needs help is entitled to receive it.

The second reason is concerned with human dignity. Charity is a great virtue for those who practise it. It also, of course, is a material benefit to those who receive it. But it may not be a spiritual benefit to them, as it is to their benefactors. To receive something as a matter of charity, of grace and favour, is liable to reinforce the recipient's feeling of lowly status. To receive something as a matter of entitlement does not have that effect. This is not to say that charity is therefore a bad thing, or even that all acts of charity should be turned into acts of justice. A distinction between justice, as the basic but mandatory virtue, and charity or generosity, as a less fundamental but nobler virtue, is probably an essential element of ethical thought. Justice is needed as the basis of social ethics; charity or generosity gives expression to the voluntary altruism which is the lifeblood of personal ethics. The ebb and flow of the tide which marks the distinction between them is an indication of the seriousness with which a society takes its ethics. The tradition which makes justice embrace help for the needy does not obliterate the distinction between justice and charity; it moves the line of distinction to a different level.

On the other hand it is also a mistake to think that the merit concept of justice has obliterated the distinction between justice and utility. It is true that a great deal of the value attributed to merit and to its reward is the value of social utility. But this is not the whole of the story.

First we should note again that the converse of reward, namely punishment, does not rest wholly on utility. The kinds of wrongdoing which make a person liable to punishment are indeed socially harmful acts, and the general purpose of the system of criminal law is the utilitarian aim of security. Again, one main purpose, if not the sole justifiable purpose, of actually inflicting punishment is the utilitarian aim of deterrence (of the offender himself and of other potential offenders) from doing similarly harmful acts in the future. Nevertheless, a non-utilitarian concept of justice comes in, too, making it a condition of liability to punishment that the person concerned has deserved it. This is a concept of desert or merit which does not depend on utility and at times conflicts with utility.

Secondly we should note that the valuing of talent, and the consequent provision of opportunity for talent, is not always, or not entirely, a utilitarian valuation. The talent of a surgeon, a design engineer, a craftsman, a shepherd, is clearly useful to society. So is the talent of a musician, a painter, an acrobat, a clown, since its exercise gives pleasure to audiences or spectators. A society which is short of surgeons, engineers, joiners, or shepherds will be prepared to finance the training of suitably endowed individuals in order to meet its own social needs. But if the same society also provides scholarships for the training of budding musicians and painters (has anybody heard of scholarships for budding acrobats or clowns?), this is not because it regards the social utility of concerts and art exhibitions as similar to that of surgery, engineering design, making furniture, or tending sheep. It provides the scholarships because it values musical or artistic talent as a flowering of the human spirit which deserves to be fostered for its own sake.

Why this particular sort of valuation should come under the concept of justice is not clear. Perhaps it is simply the result of association. Talent generally is valued for its social utility and for that reason is classed with meritorious service. Artistic talent, whose value does not lie mainly in its utility, is naturally enough classed with other talent. But I suspect that there is more to it than mere association. Self-realization consists in the development and exercise of individual gifts, and that is why modern ethical thought includes the idea of a right to education and training, if a society can afford it. Historically speaking, social utility has been more of an incentive for governments to foster universal education. But there is also the thought that education, the development of natural endowments, is the right of every individual, a claim of justice.

This right of the individual may have to be matched against utility. The Universal Declaration of Human Rights, adopted by the United Nations Organization in 1948, says in its article (no. 26) about the right to education, that elementary education should be free for all and that technical and professional education should be 'made generally available'. Available to everyone who can make use of it or only to those who can pay for it? The resources of any society are limited, and a call upon them will be made more readily for talent which is socially useful than for talent which is not, for the training of a surgeon or a computer programmer than for the training of an acrobat or a tennis-player. In terms of justice, of the right to self-development, the budding acrobat has as good a claim as the budding surgeon, but since his talent lacks social utility (other than that of giving pleasure to spectators) he cannot expect society to feel any pressing obligation about it.

Some talents are positively anti-social. A man may develop a considerable talent for burglary and cracking safes. Are we to say that even here potential talent has a claim of justice to be developed, although of course utility will turn it down flat? No, this does not follow. The moral force of any right or claim derives from the principle of ends, and that, it will be recalled, includes acting as a member of a realm of ends. The development and exercise of a talent is giving effect to a major end (object of choice), but if it is exercised so as to go against the ends of other people, then the failure to treat them as ends involves some forfeiture of your own right to be treated as an end.[4] A talent for burglary or for cracking safes is an *application* of more general capacities (of nimble movement, deft fingers, a sensitive touch, intelligent organization) which do not have to be used in a way that harms others. Justice puts in a claim for talent if it meets the ends of the individual without at the same time frustrating the ends of other people. Utility lends its support to the claim if the talent serves the ends of many and not simply those of the individual alone.

Where does all this leave the conflict between the two different concepts of progressive justice? Our discussion has shown that the merit concept of justice, whether concerned with desert or with talent, owes a good deal of its moral force to social utility. A good deal but not all. Our moral ideas about desert and talent include a non-utilitarian element, a right or entitlement of the individual, and this is something that we associate especially with the concept of justice. It seems, then, that what I

[4] Cf. p. 61 above.

have been calling the merit concept of justice is only partially a concept of justice, since it derives a good part, perhaps the major part, of its moral force from the notion of social utility, which is distinct from that of justice.

By contrast the needs concept of justice owes little of its moral force to social utility. Sometimes the meeting of need can be socially useful; for example, medical treatment for a sick worker will help him to be back at work more quickly. But this is incidental. What about medical treatment for sick people who are too old to work, or unemployment pay for people who cannot find work? The social obligation to provide for needs depends on the ends of the needy, not on the ends of society.

Likewise the equality aspect of this concept of justice has nothing to do with utility. In fact it has to be contrasted with utility-value. As we saw in Chapter 6, a utility-value can properly be attributed to a human being but that is quite distinct from valuing him as an end-in-himself. When a man is used as a means, to provide a product or service which others want, his usefulness can be rated on a scale of value, depending on the ends of others which his work satisfies. If I want a set of bookshelves I shall value highly the carpenter who can make them well, quickly, and cheaply, and I shall set a lower value on the one whose product is clumsy, delayed, and expensive. In utility-value, i.e. when rated as means, human beings are unequal; some are more valuable, more useful, than others. But when we think of human beings as ends, not as means, this kind of rating simply does not apply. The unequal rating of men as more or less valuable depends on their efficiency, as means, in meeting the ends of other people. Valuing them as ends, as beings whose own ends (desires and choices) are to be respected, obviously does not have that kind of dependence. Ends form the standard by reference to which means are rated as having more or less value. The value of means is instrumental; the value of ends determines instrumental value but is not itself determined by something else. So the inequality in value which human beings have as means does not apply to the value which they have as ends. Considered as ends, human beings do not have that inequality of value which they have as means. This is why it can truly be said that there is a fundamental equality of value among human beings, despite their obvious inequality in natural endowment or in achievement. The equality/needs concept of justice fastens upon this. While social utility can properly require differential treatment because of the unequal utility-value of different people, justice reminds us of the underlying equality of human beings as ends.

The upshot of this discussion is that the merit concept of justice owes only a part of its moral force to the idea of justice and the rest to utility, while the equality/needs concept is entirely one of justice. Does it follow from this that in cases of conflict between the two, the equality/needs concept should be given preference as the more wholehearted representative of justice? No, it does not follow. For the claim of utility, the welfare of society, is as valid a component of social ethics as is the claim of justice. Any conflict between the claim of merit and the claim of need is still a genuine conflict even if it is interpreted as a conflict between utility and justice. When this kind of conflict crops up in concrete issues of economic policy, for instance, the party which wants to give priority to merit will argue that the best way to reduce poverty is to encourage capable and enterprising people to increase the total wealth of the country. This makes some of the rich richer and so increases inequality of wealth, but it also improves the position of many of the poor. (The argument recalls Rawls's second principle of justice. He was influenced by this piece of economic theory when he put forward the principle.) The dispute has now become a difference of opinion about methods rather than aims. Those who support priority for merit are not saying that merit comes before need. They are saying that the two things go together; rewarding merit is the best way to forward the aim of helping the needy. This does not imply, however, that rewarding merit is also the best way to forward the aim of equality; the dispute between advocates of merit and advocates of equality remains a dispute about aims. Deep-seated and age-old political conflicts cannot be settled by philosophical analysis. Nevertheless philosophical analysis can do quite a lot to clarify the issues.

8 Liberty

In philosophical discussion of social and political ethics there are two rival concepts of liberty, as there are two main rival concepts of justice, but they do not have the same sort of origin. The two rival concepts of progressive justice are widely used in the moral and political thinking of ordinary life; neither of them is simply an invention of philosophers. With liberty, however, the position is different. One of the two rival concepts is the commonsense meaning of freedom or liberty, while the other is a peculiar meaning largely invented by theorists because of their objections to the commonsense idea.

The plain meaning of freedom is the absence of restraint. If we say that John Smith is free to leave the country, we mean that there is no bar on his leaving; there is no law or administrative procedure which will stop him from leaving if he wants to. Freedom is always freedom *from* some possible restraint and freedom *to* do what you want or choose to do.

The idea has different applications (not different meanings), and it is sometimes important to be clear about these. Freedom of choice (or free will) is different from social freedom (or liberty). When a man is free to choose between alternative courses of action, this means that he is not prevented by physical or psychological causes from having two genuine options open to him. For example, one might ask whether John Smith, in the light of his meagre savings or his personal history, really has a free choice of staying in this country or emigrating to Canada. If he does not have the money to pay the fare, it is simply not open to him to opt for emigration. If he does have the money but is so strongly attached to his native England that he cannot bear to leave, then perhaps again it is not really open to him to choose emigration. But suppose he does have a genuine choice; he has the money and he has no psychological inhibitions about leaving. Suppose further that he decides to emigrate. He has exercised his freedom of choice. There is now the further question whether he is free (has the social freedom) to give effect to his choice. Having chosen to emigrate, is he free to carry out that choice? If he *is* free, this means that he will not be restrained or prevented by the action of some other person or persons. If John Smith does not have a valid passport, he will be prevented from boarding the aircraft by the officials who examine passports. If he has a valid passport (and so is free to *leave*) but has a criminal record which the Canadian authorities regard as an objection to his settling in Canada, then he will be prevented by Canadian officials from entering their country or from remaining there for more than a limited period.

I have called the second kind of freedom 'social freedom' because it is the absence of restraint by other people. (A man who is locked up in prison has his freedom restrained by bolts and bars, but it is the actions of police officers which have brought him to the prison and the actions of prison officers which have locked the gates.) The word 'liberty' in English is normally used only of social freedom, freedom from restraint by the action of other persons; it is not used (in modern English) of freedom to choose, freedom from restraint by physical or psychological causes upon choosing between options.

Freedom of choice poses a difficult philosophical problem which I shall discuss in Chapters 9 and 10. The problem is whether there is such a thing as freedom of choice or free will. Social freedom is quite different. There is no philosophical problem whether social freedom can exist, but there is a problem for political theory about the extent to which social freedom should be allowed.

Complete social freedom contradicts itself unless people have nothing to do with each other. To be socially free is to face no restrictions on doing as you like. But if Tom does just as he likes with no thought of the effect on his neighbours Dick and Harry, he is apt to prevent Dick and Harry from doing as they like. For instance, if Tom likes to play his electric guitar at 2 a.m. when Dick likes to be asleep, Tom's freedom to do as he likes interferes with Dick's freedom to do as *he* likes. If there were no laws limiting our freedom to do as we like, we should in one sense be completely free, free from all legal restraint. But on a broader understanding of the situation we should have little freedom, little real opportunity to do as we like, for our freedom would be restricted by the unbridled actions of other people. We should be at the mercy of any man's whim or greed, and none of us would be strong enough or clever enough to fend off all attackers. Complete legal freedom for all means little effective freedom for anyone.

Obviously, then, social freedom or liberty must be restricted if it is to be effective. The problem for political theory is how far the restriction should go. Where should the line be drawn between the liberty of the individual and the authority of the State? A political theorist who puts liberty high on his scale of values will advocate the greatest possible amount of freedom that is compatible with similar freedom for other people. The primary function of the State, he will tell us, is to protect the liberties of all its citizens. To do this it needs to limit liberty but the limitation should be as small as possible. A political theorist who sets more store by security and is fearful of the dangers of liberty will be ready to enlarge the scope of State authority and to narrow down the amount of individual liberty. These two types of theorist disagree on the relative importance to be attached to liberty and security, and so they disagree on where the line should be drawn between liberty and authority. But they agree that liberty and authority are opposed to each other; more of the one implies less of the other.

There is, however, a tradition of philosophical thought about politics which denies that liberty and authority are opposed to each other. This has produced the second concept of liberty, the one which is a rival to the commonsense concept. It arises from the same kind of attitude that advocates a great measure of authority for the State: a concern for security and an acute awareness of the dangers of letting people do as they like. But it refuses to accept the commonsense view that being allowed to do as one likes is liberty. Liberty is an honoured name. Everyone is in favour of it. If you say that liberty is a bad thing, you will not get much support. And since liberty is everywhere honoured, there must be a sound reason for it. Genuine liberty, the idea that deserves to be honoured, must be something different from the misplaced idea of liberty as being allowed to do as one likes. Consequently this tradition of thought, which favours a maximum of authority, tries to argue that genuine liberty marches hand in hand with authority.

The argument is a fairly elaborate one and needs to be spelled out in some detail. But first it will be convenient to find a name for this peculiar concept of liberty which goes dead against the commonsense meaning of the term. Sir Isaiah Berlin[1] calls the two concepts 'positive' and 'negative' liberty, but these names are misleading. The commonsense concept does define freedom negatively as the absence of restraint but it has a positive aspect too; the commonsense idea of freedom is always freedom *to* do something as well as freedom *from* some restraint. John Stuart Mill, the most admired and the most criticized advocate of this concept of liberty, finds the chief value of liberty in the development of individuality,[2] surely a positive idea. What the critics of the commonsense concept deplore is not the absence of a positive aspect but the *character* of its positive aspect. At the beginning of this chapter I said that freedom, as commonly understood, is always freedom *from* some restraint and always

[1] *Two Concepts of Liberty* (1958), reprinted in *Four Essays on Liberty* (1969).
[2] *On Liberty*, chap. 3.

freedom *to* do what you want or choose to do. It is important to remember the alternatives 'want or choose', because there are times when a man claims liberty of conscience and chooses to do what he believes is right, although unpopular and so liable to bring unpleasant consequences for him. In these circumstances what he does is not what he *wants* or would *like* to do. It would be pleasanter for him to follow the crowd. But he *chooses* to do otherwise because he thinks it right. Such a situation is, however, fairly exceptional. Generally speaking, liberty or social freedom is freedom to do as you want. This is what the critics of the commonsense concept deplore. If the positive aspect of liberty is freedom to do what one *wants*, then the value of liberty depends on the value of satisfying desires. The critics object to this because they think that the value of liberty is high and the value of satisfying desire is low. They want liberty to depend on something more exalted than desire. The difference between their view and the commonsense concept is not a difference between positive and negative but a difference between high-flown notions and down-to-earth notions.

I shall refer to their view as the idealist concept of liberty because, in its fully fledged form, it was held by nineteenth-century philosophers known as Objective Idealists. The name 'Idealism' in this connection has nothing to do with the holding of ideals. In general philosophy the term 'Idealism' is used for the theory that the contents of the mind ('ideas') are real while matter is not. This seems a very odd theory, though the arguments for it are not negligible. However, this contention, which the Objective Idealists of the nineteenth century (Hegel and his followers) shared with earlier Idealists such as Bishop Berkeley, has little to do with their concept of freedom. What Berlin calls the 'positive' concept of liberty began with Plato in the ancient world and was developed to some degree by Rousseau in the eighteenth century. It was then taken over and developed further by Hegel and his followers. It is more closely connected with their theory of ethics than with their idealist theory of metaphysics.

In the ordinary way we would say that liberty and authority are opposed to each other. Liberty is (usually) doing as you like. Authority prevents people from doing just as they like; it requires them to do this and forbids them to do that. We have seen the point of having such restrictions. If the enjoyment of *some* freedom is to be protected, there must be a restriction of further freedom which would otherwise make the first kind of freedom impossible. A measure of authority is necessary to protect a measure of freedom. But, of course, absolute authority would leave us with no freedom at all; no authority results in no freedom, and absolute authority results in no freedom. At least it does so if we understand by freedom the possibility of doing as you like.

The idealist concept of freedom puts forward the paradoxical thesis that authority enhances freedom; not just that limited authority *protects* limited freedom (we have seen the truth of this), but that the following of authority *is* true or genuine freedom, that a man can be 'forced to be free'.[3] Obviously this must be using the word 'freedom' in a queer sense; and certainly the idealist theory rejects the commonsense view that freedom is doing as you like.

In fact it begins from that denial. The commonsense idea is that freedom is the absence of restraint on doing as you wish. But this, says the philosophical idealist, means acting from desire, and to act from desire is not a good thing. The good thing is to do what is morally right and to act from a sense of duty. Duty and desire can conflict, and if a man, in such a situation, gives way to desire, he is not doing what is right and good, nor is he acting freely; he is in bondage to his desire. Think of someone who is an alcoholic or a drug addict. He has a craving for whisky or heroin. He knows that it is ruining his health and that he ought to stop; but he cannot. Is he not enslaved by his desire for drink or drugs? If he is forcibly prevented from having access to drink or drugs, and eventually his craving dies down for lack of sustenance, has he not been freed from a terrible taskmaster? And if you agree to that, can one draw any firm line between the alcoholic and the man who regularly has his pint or his dram? Can one draw any clear line between the addict who takes LSD and the addict who smokes tobacco? Are there not many smokers who think they ought to give it up but cannot? Are they not the slaves of tobacco as much as the alcoholic is the slave of drink?

Having gone that far, the argument then asks whether we can draw a firm line between addiction and giving in to *any* desire. We cannot draw a clear line between the alcoholic and the man who has his pint a day and who would feel deprived without it. We cannot draw a clear line between him and the man who likes to drink from time to time. Doing what you like, acting from desire, is the road to bondage, says the idealist. The only true freedom is to act rationally, from the thought of what is right.

The idealist thinks that his argument is confirmed by considerations of free will. Many philosophers agree that the motivation of desire acts in a deterministic fashion. This goes along with the things that I have just been talking about. An alcoholic, or an addict to drugs or tobacco, cannot help what he does. He just cannot exert enough will-power to resist temptation. Now if you agree that no clear line can be drawn between giving in to an addictive craving and being motivated by any ordinary desire, and if you also agree that the former is necessitated behaviour, it seems to follow that the latter must be necessitated too. So all conduct

[3] The phrase comes from Rousseau, *Du contrat social*, I.7.

motivated by *desire* is necessitated or determined. Well, in a situation of moral choice a man has free will. To say that he *ought* to do something is to imply that he *can* do it, indeed that he has a choice whether to do it or not. A situation of moral choice is often one where duty and desire conflict. Then if motivation by desire is necessitated, and if moral choice is free, it seems to follow that the freedom of choice must attach only to conduct motivated by the sense of duty. The conclusion appears to be that acting from reason, from the thought of right and wrong, is free, while acting from desire is unfree.

This conclusion is much the same as the one I discussed a few moments ago. The point is that the idealist philosopher assumes from it that freedom of choice is the same thing as the freedom or liberty which comes into social and political discussion. Freedom, in the social and political sense, is contrasted with slavery or bondage. Free will is contrasted with being necessitated. Since we can speak of being enslaved by desire, it is natural to suppose that its opposite, freedom of choice, is the essence of social freedom.

So the idealist philosopher concludes that doing as you like is not true freedom; it is a form of bondage, being necessitated by desire. True freedom is free will, which can be exercised only when a man does what is right, when he is motivated by reason, by the thought of duty.

Up to this point the argument does not have any special *political* implications. But now we must go on. It is a commonplace that people often do not choose to do what is right. It is also a commonplace that many people often do not know what is right. These two commonplaces can be connected if you accept a view which has been tempting to a number of philosophers ever since the time of Socrates. It is the view that if a man knows what is right, he is *bound* to do it in the sense that he will inevitably do it. How could he not? It would be irrational not to do it, and he must be a rational man since he knows what is right. So you have the conclusion that a man who fails to do what is right must have gone wrong through ignorance. He does not know what is right; he must think that what he is doing is the right thing to do, but he is mistaken.

This view that wrongdoing is the effect of ignorance was a natural one for Greek philosophers to take, since a familiar Greek term for wrongdoing could also mean missing the mark, making a mistake. Socrates took an intellectualist view of ethics; virtue is knowledge (he meant the knowledge of how to achieve happiness), and vice is ignorance. Plato gave a political slant to this intellectualist theory of ethics. Knowledge or wisdom is confined to a few. Ignorance, or at least an absence of what is properly called knowledge, is the lot of the masses. So the masses cannot achieve virtue on their own; they cannot know what is right, and they cannot do what is right if left to themselves. The way has to be pointed out to them by the wise. Virtue for the masses lies in doing as they are told by their wise rulers.

The fruits of a philosophy can be more powerful than its roots. Neither Rousseau nor Hegel held the intellectualist theory of ethics that came more naturally to Greek thinkers; and Rousseau, though not Hegel, differed from Plato also in his political sympathies. Rousseau was a democrat; in some ways he is the most fervent advocate of democracy to be found in the whole history of political thought. Yet he was deeply affected by Plato's political ideas as they applied to freedom, and Rousseau's view of political freedom became more powerful still in the hands of Hegel, who was not inhibited by any democratic leanings.

The line of argument that I set out a little earlier led to the conclusion that freedom is not doing what you like but is doing what is right; it is not following desire but is following reason. Now add to that the view that wisdom is the prerogative of the few. The masses do not know what is right. So far as law and the State are concerned, it seems plain common sense to say that most people have to be told what to do and what not to do. The ordinary man does not realize what effects his action may have on other people, or at any rate he does not think about it. Left to himself he will pollute the countryside and the atmosphere. If he fancies some fish, he will not reflect that netting the whole fish population of a pond will leave no fish for others, or for himself next year. If he wants wood, he will cut down the trees and will not think that this may cause erosion of the soil. The ordinary man does not know these things or does not think about them. He needs to be told what not to do in the interests of other people, of future generations, and indeed of his own future. In many matters of social concern, ordinary people are ignorant and have to be told what is right.

But now, if to do what is right and to follow reason is to be free, one can argue that laws and governors, who tell us what is rational and the right thing to do in social matters, are thereby making us free. The wise man who knows these things for himself and acts off his own bat is certainly a free man, he is exercising free choice of moral action. But the ordinary unwise man, who does not know for himself, who has to be told what to do, who at times has to be *ordered* to do it, and if necessary *made* to do it under the threat of sanctions, he too, according to this line of argument, is made *free* by the law, for he is made to do what is right and rational; and if he has to be forced by sanctions, then he is 'forced to be free'.

It is a paradoxical conclusion, yet you can see that the argument which leads up to it is complex and at each step quite persuasive – until we are pulled up sharp by the strange conclusion. The idealist theory of freedom is not just a theory, a finely woven cobweb that is a marvel to look at but carries no weight. It has had a strong influence on practical political movements. While it appears to have a certain profundity, I think it is profoundly mistaken. I shall give three criticisms of it.

(1) From the fact that *some* desires enslave, it does not follow that all desires enslave. You might just as well argue that because some people have red noses, it follows that all people have red noses. But what about the argument that you cannot draw a firm line anywhere between addiction and an ordinary desire? This is true, but it does not mean that there is no difference between one end of the scale and the other. Take my analogy of the people with red noses. Suppose you line up a lot of people on a cold day; you put those with red noses at one end, those with blue noses at the other end, and then arrange the people in between according to whether their noses approach more nearly to being red or being blue. If you then walk along the parade, there is no definite point at which you can say 'Here the red noses stop'. When you come to Tom, one third of the way along the line, will you say that his nose is red, or purple, or reddish-purple, or purplish-red? The difficulty is clearer still if you get an artist to paint a surface merging imperceptibly from red at one side to blue at the other. There is no place at which you can draw a firm line and say 'This is where red comes to an end'. But it would be quite silly to conclude, because of this, that the blue noses (or the blue parts of the painting) at the other end are really red.

The same thing goes for desire. It is perfectly true that you cannot draw a firm line between desires that enslave and those that do not. All the same, there is an undoubted difference between the alcoholic's craving for a glass of whisky and an ordinary desire for a cup of tea or a glass of water when thirsty. Anyone who has ever formed the habit of smoking knows that there is a difference between the feeling that he must have a cigarette and the ordinary desire to have a meal when hungry, a drink when thirsty, a walk when feeling brisk, and a rest when feeling tired. Although we cannot draw a line just here or just there, our everyday experience shows a clear difference between those desires that we call cravings or addictions and those that we do not. There is therefore no good reason to say that all desires enslave or that all action motivated by desire is necessitated.

(2) The idealist theory fails to distinguish freedom of choice from social freedom. A man has freedom of choice or free will if he is able to *choose* between alternatives, as contrasted with the drug addict or the alcoholic, who is driven along the one way willy-nilly and has no choice. Now a man may have free will but not be *allowed* to give effect to his choice. For

instance, if I am not an alcoholic, I can choose whether or not to have a glass of whisky after my dinner. But if I decide to have a glass, and if I then find that somebody has locked up the whisky bottle and has taken away the key, then I am prevented from acting upon my choice; I am not free to carry out the choice that I have made. Similarly a prohibition law takes away a man's freedom to drink, but that is different from a psychological inhibition (perhaps the result of religious upbringing) which makes him incapable of accepting strong drink when it is available.

It is possible to believe that there is no such thing as free will, but this does not prevent one from recognizing that some people have more social freedom than others. To take a pertinent example from the history of political theory, Hobbes and J.S. Mill both denied the existence of free will; nevertheless each of them was very much concerned with questions of social freedom, what it is, why it is valued, what are its dangers, what should be its limits. Although these two philosophers were agreed in thinking that free will is a myth, they were very far indeed from agreement on social freedom. Hobbes was in favour of as little freedom as possible; Mill was in favour of as much freedom as possible. The dispute between them is of the highest importance for political theory and political practice. When the idealist theory of freedom confuses social freedom with freedom of the will, it simply obscures the issues about social freedom.

(3) Within the notion of free will itself the idealist theory goes wrong in its supposition that freedom applies only to the choice of right action. When a choice has to be made, the person choosing is confronted with two or more possibilities. To say that he can choose between them is to say that each possibility is open to him; he can do either. He is free to select either the one or the other. In a situation of moral choice, therefore, an agent is free to do either what is right or what is wrong. If you say that only one of these is a free action, you are really denying that there is freedom of choice. The idealist theory does not really believe in free will at all. It says that the man who follows desire is necessitated by desire. And what about the man who follows his sense of duty? He is not necessitated by desire, but having got himself free from bondage to desire, there is only one thing he can do, follow his sense of duty. If there is only one thing that he *can* do, then he *must* do it. He is free from the bondage of desire, but he is subject to the necessity of reason or duty. To say that he is free, that he has achieved a true or higher freedom, is only to say that he is free from necessitation by desire. He is not free from *all* necessitation; the one necessitation is replaced by another.

The force of this criticism can be seen more clearly if we turn back to the social application of the idealist theory. According to the theory, a man who is not himself highly rational can be put in the position of the rational man by the law. Take the case of the drug addict again. When the law prevents him from satisfying his desire for more drugs, it removes the constraint of desire; it does not allow him to remain enslaved to desire. True enough, but does it therefore follow that he becomes a free man, a free agent? Not a bit of it. What happens is that one constraint is replaced by another. The man is no longer constrained by his craving to act in one way; instead he is constrained by the law to act in a different way.

We must acknowledge, however, that the long-term effect of the law can be to restore the drug addict's will-power. The law prevents him from having access to drugs, and in time (with luck and suitable medical care) the craving disappears through lack of sustenance, so that the former addict may become a normal human being again, able to resist temptation of his own volition. So the law can be part of the means of restoring his power of choice, his free will. In this sense the constraints of law can help to make him free. There is that element of truth in the idealist theory. We sometimes do need to be helped to stand on our own feet. We are helped by medical care, by education, and sometimes by law. We are helped to reach self-reliance, the development of personality. Perhaps this is more important than the freedom of doing as we like. One can argue, as J.S. Mill does, that freedom is valuable just because it permits the development of personality.

Nevertheless it is also important not to confuse different things. Constraint by law may sometimes be part of the means whereby freedom of choice can be restored or strengthened. This does not imply that being forced by the law is *the same thing* as exercising free choice. Still less does it imply that either of these things is the same as social freedom. It is only too easy for the idealist concept of freedom to be used by an authoritarian regime so as to justify repression in the name of freedom.

Free will and determinism

9 Concepts of science

Everyday experience leads us to suppose that we often have a choice between alternative courses of action. The choice is not a wide one. We know that there are lots of things which we might contemplate doing but which are simply not open to us for all sorts of reasons. One cannot jump over the moon; it is physically impossible. One cannot square the circle; it is logically impossible. I cannot run a four-minute mile, though some people can. So it would not make sense for me to talk of choosing to do these things. I might wish that I could run a four-minute mile, but since I know (or believe) that I cannot, it would be logically absurd for me to talk of choosing or deciding to run a four-minute mile. Often we do not know the limits of our capabilities and we may suppose that we have a choice when in fact we do not. For example, a man who has frequently walked thirty miles a day in his youth, may think himself still capable of it in middle age and set out to do such a walk but find that he cannot manage it. On the other hand we occasionally underrate our capacities and suppose that something is not within our power when in fact it is. The middle-aged man may think that he is no longer capable of the thirty-mile walk but, when cajoled into seeing how far he can go, may find that he can do the thirty miles after all.

As we learn more about ourselves and about human beings generally, we alter our views concerning the area in which we think there is a genuine choice between alternatives. In particular, the development of psychological knowledge shows that some types of people (and all of us at some times) are more subject to inner compulsions than we had supposed. We all understand the effect that physical pain or deprivation can have on choice: torture can break the will of its victims, depriving them altogether of the power to defy their captors; less radically, starvation reduces will-power, making it much more difficult, for instance, to resist the temptation to steal a loaf of bread if opportunity offers. Psychologists tell us that some people find it even more difficult to resist the temptation to steal because they are suffering from a neurosis called kleptomania. As a result, there have been changes in ideas about the proper way to deal with such people: theft by a kleptomaniac calls for psychiatric treatment rather than imprisonment. Courts of law nowadays are ready to hear evidence of uncontrollable impulse or diminished responsibility and, if persuaded, to modify verdicts or sentences.

The starving man and the kleptomaniac certainly have *less* choice than the normal man. Is it true to say that they have *no* choice? There is no doubt that torture can remove choice altogether for most people (though there do seem to be a few exceptions). The effect of starvation is less extreme; some hunger strikers are able to refuse food even at the point of death, and a captor who wanted information would not think much of starvation instead of torture as a method of trying to extract it. A starving man who does steal a loaf of bread is unlikely to say or think that he literally has no alternative, though he will expect others to agree that it is not a tolerable alternative. What about the kleptomaniac? It looks as if he has less freedom of choice than the starving thief, but is it literally true that he has no alternative, that his neurosis has a strictly compulsive force? A kleptomaniac presumably does not steal when he knows that a policeman or a store detective is looking on. If so, this means that the psychological neurosis can be inhibited by another psychological factor. It then becomes pertinent to ask whether the neurosis could not be inhibited by a different psychological factor, a strong feeling that it is wrong to steal. In other words, is resistance to temptation extremely difficult for the kleptomaniac but not absolutely impossible?

At any rate the kleptomaniac, like the starving thief, does not have the degree of free choice that we commonly attribute to a psychologically normal or a well-fed man. It was certainly a mistake to think, as people did in the old days, that anyone who steals is equally capable of choosing not to steal if he just makes an effort. But if modern scientific knowledge shows that ordinary unsophisticated opinion can be mistaken about some types of thief, is it not possible, indeed likely, that advances in scientific knowledge will disclose more mistakes in ordinary unsophisticated opinion? Is ordinary unsophisticated opinion a reliable guide at all? Should we not put greater trust in the methods of science?

Once we ask that kind of question, the philosophical problem of free will and determinism begins to emerge. Scientific explanation is usually a matter of understanding the causes of phenomena. The physical sciences are commonly taken to be the model of scientific procedure at its best, and in the physical sciences to give a causal explanation of an event is to show that it is an instance of a necessary law. For example, we may ask why a stick partly immersed in water looks as if it bends at an angle in the place where it meets the surface of the water. Physics gives us the answer in the laws of refraction. The cause of the apparent bending is that rays of light are bent when they pass from air to a denser medium. Snell's law of the refraction of light gives us a universal statement that the rays of light are bent towards the vertical in a constant ratio. So if we want to know why the oar of a boat looks as if it were bent to an angle of about 20°, a physicist will tell us that this is a necessary consequence of Snell's law. Well, if that kind of thing is the model of scientific explanation, and if (as appears to be the case) scientific explanation can be applied to human behaviour, then human behaviour, like the behaviour of physical objects, must be subject to necessary laws. The torturer's victim discloses secret information because he must; the pain of the torture forces him to speak up. The kleptomaniac steals because he must; his neurosis compels him to do so. It is true that the kleptomaniac does not steal when he knows that a detective is watching him, but then this simply means that a counteracting force has been stronger than the neurosis. Like everybody else, the kleptomaniac is afraid of being imprisoned, and that fear is sharpest when the chance of being caught is very high. So if he knows that a detective is watching, his fear of the legal penalties is stronger than the force of his neurotic impulse to steal. His behaviour can still be compared with that of a physical object. If you place a magnet on one side of an iron filing, the filing will fly towards the magnet; it must do so. But if you make the iron filing subject to opposed forces, placing magnets of similar strength on opposite sides of the filing at similar distances, the filing will appear to waver and will then move towards the magnet which exerts the stronger force. Social scientists do not know as much about the forces which act on human nature as physicists do about the forces which act on pieces of matter, so that the explanations of social science are far from complete. But in principle the analogy seems, at first sight, to be acceptable. Although we usually do not have adequate and accurate knowledge of the causes of human behaviour, there must in fact be such causes. That is to say, human actions are necessarily determined by their causes, but we are usually ignorant of what those causes are, and in consequence we are led to suppose that human actions are not necessarily caused.

This is the view of determinism, the theory that human actions, like all other events, are determined, necessitated, by their causes. It is to be contrasted with libertarianism, the view that some (not by any means all) human actions are freely chosen, that they might not have been chosen, that an alternative might have been chosen without any change in the preceding circumstances. According to libertarianism, therefore, such actions are not determined by their preceding conditions; they are strongly influenced but not necessitated.

The problem of free will and determinism, in the form most relevant to modern ideas, arises from an apparent conflict between the presuppositions of science and the presuppositions of practical thinking in everyday life (especially about ethics) and in the law. For an earlier age, substantially the same problem arose from an apparent conflict between the presuppositions of biblical theology and those of everyday practical thinking, especially in ethics. According to biblical theology, God is omnipotent, omniscient, and unchanging. Since he is the omnipotent creator of everything in the universe, and since he always acts consistently, it seems to follow that everything which happens is (ultimately) caused by God and could not have been made any different by the choice of men. Furthermore, since God is omniscient, he knows the future as well as the past, and from this it seems to follow that what will happen in the future is already fixed, unalterable by any choice that human beings may make. Biblical theology therefore appears to imply determinism.

This conclusion poses difficulties for theology itself and not simply for mundane ideas about ethics and human action generally. For biblical religion also includes a belief in human free will and human responsibility. If God is the (ultimate) cause of everything which happens, then God must be responsible for what men do; but biblical religion holds that men are also responsible for their deeds, that they can choose to do good or evil, and that God is not responsible if men wilfully choose to do evil. Again, a firm acceptance of theological determinism, as in the Calvinist doctrine of predestination, appears to produce a conflict with the further presupposition of biblical theology that God is perfectly good and just: if God has these ethical attributes, how can he predestine some men to heaven and others to hell, irrespective of what they do in the course of their lives?

These difficulties we may leave to the theologians. The point to which I wish to draw attention is that the problem raised for free will by biblical theology is in principle the same as the problem raised by science. In each case there are two aspects of the difficulty, one about causation, the other about knowledge of the future. With theology the first point is that there is a universal, consistent, causal agency for everything which happens; and the second point is that the future is foreknown. With science the first point is that scientific method assumes a universal, consistent, system of causation for everything which happens; and the second point is that the future is often predictable. The aims of science, it might be said, are precisely to discover the causal laws which explain phenomena and to make predictions. This partial coincidence of outlook in the presuppositions of biblical theology and of modern science is not as surprising as it appears at first sight. It is due to the fact that both of them impose a *unified* frame of reference upon the phenomena of experience. Monotheism unifies with a single causal agency in place of the many separate agencies, each responsible for some part of the world, postulated by polytheistic religions. Modern science unifies with a single interconnected system of causal laws in place of *ad hoc* explanations and predictions of particular types of event such as can be reached by a shrewd set of farmers or sailors who are prepared to learn from experience. As a matter of history the unifying outlook of modern science was probably inherited from the unified vision of biblical religion.

The two main arguments for determinism are those that I have briefly touched upon in comparing the apparent implications of science with those of biblical theology. First, every event has a cause. This means, so it is said, that every event is necessitated. Human actions are a species of events and so human actions are necessitated. Secondly, future actions can often be predicted from knowledge of a person's character and circumstances. This, it is alleged, is confirmatory evidence that those future actions are determined by the relevant preceding conditions.

The case for free will has most commonly been supported by two arguments of different character. The first is a simple appeal to experience. As I remarked in Chapter 8, anyone who has ever formed the habit of smoking is conscious of a recognizable difference between the feeling that he must have a cigarette and an ordinary desire to have a meal when hungry. He feels compelled by the one but not by the other. Along with such experience of the different strengths of different desires, there goes experience of deciding or choosing to do something. When the habitual smoker says he 'must' have a cigarette and lights up, he may well feel that he has no choice in the matter. When he decides to have tea rather than coffee for breakfast, he neither feels compelled nor feels any difficulty in making his choice. But if, after smoking the cigarette that he feels he 'must' have, he then feels that he would like to follow it with another, he may find that he can resist the temptation, at least for the time being. It is not an easy matter, like choosing tea rather than coffee for breakfast because he has been told that coffee produces acidity. To resist the temptation to smoke another cigarette, he has to make a conscious effort. But still, he can manage it. It is a psychological analogue to managing, with some physical effort, to lift a heavy ladder, as contrasted with the easy job of picking up a hammer and with the (for him) impossible job of lifting a 50-kilo sack of coal. The second argument is that freedom of choice is presupposed by the idea of moral obligation: 'ought' implies 'can'; to say or think that one ought to do something is to imply that one can do it and also that one need not. This does not prove that free will exists; it tries to show only that free will is required by morality. If someone is prepared to deny the truth of our moral ideas, he can be unmoved by this argument. A thoroughgoing determinist will indeed say both that the ordinary interpretation of experience is unreliable and that our usual ideas about morality are mistaken.

Before going further, however, we must note that some philosophers have claimed that the supposed problem of free will versus determinism rests on a misunderstanding. Both doctrines, they say, if properly understood, are true and are quite compatible with each other. This way of dealing with the matter may be called the compatibility thesis.

According to the compatibility thesis, determinism must be accepted because it is certainly true that every event has a cause. On the other hand, the idea of freedom must also be accepted because there is a valid distinction between action which is free or voluntary and action which is compelled or involuntary. The two views are compatible, however, it is alleged, because the distinction between the voluntary and the involuntary is not a distinction between the uncaused and the caused. All actions are caused, but some have internal causes and others have external causes. If you stay in your study because you want to do so, you stay of your own free will; you act voluntarily. If you stay in your study because somebody has locked the door and taken away the key, you stay under compulsion; you act involuntarily. That is a perfectly proper distinction. But it does not affect the truth of the statement that in either case your action has a cause. When you remain voluntarily, the cause is your own desire to remain. When you remain involuntarily, the cause is the limitation placed on your movements by the locked door. When the cause is internal, a desire of the agent, we say that he acts voluntarily, of his own free will or wish. When the cause is external and happens to clash with what the agent wants to do, we say that he acts involuntarily or is compelled. It is perfectly possible to act voluntarily and yet from a necessitating cause. The proper distinction to be drawn, according to this account, is a distinction between freedom and compulsion, not between freedom and necessity.

The compatibility thesis does not give to the libertarian all that he asks for. It does not agree that human beings have a special capacity of free will which no other animal has. A dog, like a man, may stay in a room voluntarily or involuntarily. Indeed Hobbes (who was, so far as I know, the originator of the compatibility thesis) pointed out that a similar distinction can be drawn for inanimate objects: we say that a river flows freely down to the sea and that it is not free to flow when it is stopped by a dam; yet when it flows freely it does so of necessity.[1] In this case the cause of the action called free is not in the river itself but in the laws of gravity, but this natural or normal cause is contrasted with the hindrance

[1] *Leviathan*, chap. 21.

to normal motion provided by the dam. (The idiom of 'free flow' or 'free fall', applied to material things, was used long before the days of Newtonian gravitational theory and is probably rooted in the idea of Aristotelian science that a falling body has an innate tendency to seek its 'natural' place. On that sort of view, the cause of the 'natural' motion *is* internal.)

The compatibility thesis, then, does not give the libertarian all that he asks for. Does it nevertheless give him all that he needs? It does not. Libertarianism must accommodate the belief that actions which are freely chosen might not have been chosen, that it was genuinely open to the agent to have made an alternative choice. The compatibility thesis does not allow for freedom of choice; it allows for freedom of action (what in Chapter 8 I have called social freedom). There is no problem of reconciling determinism with freedom of action, as Hobbes's example of the free-flowing river makes clear. I have called Hobbes the originator of the compatibility thesis but he, unlike later holders of it, was quite clear that he denied the truth of free will. He said that liberty was compatible with necessity but he knew very well that the liberty which he meant was social liberty. (The chapter which I quoted in note 1 above is entitled 'Of the Liberty of Subjects'.) In the controversy between free will and determinism, the compatibility thesis simply adopts the view of determinism.

Let us now look at the two main arguments for determinism. The first is the more important. It contains four steps. (1) Every event has a cause. (2) This implies that every event is necessitated. (3) Actions are a species of events. (4) Therefore every action is necessitated.

In the context of epistemological inquiry, it would be necessary to ask how we know, and whether in fact we do know, that every event has a cause. But in the context of moral philosophy, it is proper to accept the truth of this universal statement. At any rate its truth is generally presupposed in science and the success of scientific method contributes much to the persuasive force of determinism. Someone may ask whether Heisenberg's 'principle of indeterminacy' in nuclear physics does not deny the truth of the statement that *every* event has a cause, but let us leave that question over for the moment. It is more clearly relevant to the second step in the argument for determinism. That second step is the crucial one and needs to be examined with care. If it is sound, the rest of the argument follows straightforwardly. For the third step simply says that actions are a species of events, and this is certainly true. There may be more to an action than there is to a physical event, but an action at least includes an event. So if the second step in the determinist argument is sound, the third step gives no ground for questioning the conclusion that all actions are necessitated. Let us now turn to the crucial second step.

The second step is the claim that 'Every event has a cause' implies 'Every event is necessitated'. The idea here is that the link between cause and effect always has the character which it has in classical mechanics; the causal explanation of an event lies in showing that the event falls under a universal necessary law. If you ask why an apple, when detached from its tree, falls to the ground, or why the seas are subject to the ebb and flow of tides, or why the earth describes an elliptical orbit round the sun, Newton's law of gravitation gives a satisfactory explanation. A commonsense understanding of Newton's law includes the idea of gravity as a force which 'pulls' the apple towards the centre of the earth, the tides towards the moon, and the earth towards the sun. Nowadays, when there is a more sophisticated notion of gravity in relativity theory, we are told that it is too crude to think of gravity as 'pulling' in the way that a horse might pull a cart. But the important thing is that the apple must fall, the tides must ebb and flow, the earth must move around the sun; these events are consequences of the universal law described by Newton. Whether or not scientists think of gravity as a 'force' of 'attraction' or as something else (such as a property of space), what matters is that the phenomena falling under the law of gravitation admit of no exceptions to the rule. The regularity which the law describes is a *universal* regularity. This is the characteristic mark of a scientific *law*.

In the physical sciences, causal explanation takes the form of showing that the event to be explained is an instance of a law, a universal regularity. It is not at all clear that the same thing is true of causal explanation in the biological sciences. But for our purpose, the discussion of determinism, the question is whether it is true of causal explanation in the social sciences, the sciences of human behaviour. Determinism in fact consists in transferring the model of causal explanation used in the physical sciences to the explanation of human behaviour. It assumes that explanation in social science is in principle the same as explanation in physical science.

We should note at this point that Heisenberg's principle of indeterminacy says that even in physics the usual model does not always apply. The exception concerns the behaviour of electrons, and Heisenberg's principle says that there are circumstances in which it is not possible to obtain a precise result in observing two related phenomena (e.g. the position and the momentum of an electron) at the same time; measuring the one introduces an 'indeterminacy' in the other. Physicists are not all agreed on the proper way to interpret this principle. It may mean that the actual physical property is not precisely determined, or it may simply mean that the (precisely determined) property cannot be observed or measured with precise accuracy. If the latter interpretation were correct, the exception would not be so radical. But even if the more radical interpretation is correct, this development in modern physics does not afford a positive supporting argument for free will. Indeterminacy in the properties of electrons does not imply that electrons have any *choice* in the matter. The relevance of Heisenberg's principle is that this branch of physical science can continue to make progress without having to rely on the search for, and discovery of, universal necessary laws. The nuclear physicist is able to work out a high degree of probability for the regular behaviour of the electrons with which he is concerned. The regularity is less than 100 per cent but it is still enough to be used as a significant datum in scientific work. Even in physics scientific work can be done with regularities that are not universal.

In the social sciences, so far as I can see, this is *always* the case. Much of the work done in social studies can properly claim to follow scientific methods, but this does not mean that these studies have discovered causal *laws* in the strict sense of that term. The word 'law' is used from time to time but I cannot think of a single instance which really is an established *universal* regularity. The social sciences are not necessarily the worse for that. Sound scientific work can certainly be done with regularities of less than 100 per cent, and whether or not I am right in saying that universal laws cannot be found in the social sciences, it is perfectly clear that in general these studies build upon regularities which are not universal.

The discipline among the social studies which has the strongest claim to be called a science is economics. Economists have used, and sometimes still do use, the word 'law' to describe some of their general principles. But they do not suppose that these principles apply in every single case. The principles describe strong trends or tendencies, what usually happens. The same sort of thing is true of economic 'models' such as the hypothesis of a system of perfect competition. No economist supposes that his model is an exact representation of economic reality, but if it fits reasonably well it is a useful device for working out consequences.

Take any example you like of an economic 'law'. For the sake of simplicity, take the law of supply and demand. This says that prices rise when demand exceeds supply, and prices fall when supply exceeds demand. In general, of course, this is perfectly true. On Saturday afternoon the greengrocer in a market will reduce the price of perishable fruits which are still left on his hands, because he wants to get rid of them before the weekend closure; supply exceeds demand at the earlier price, and so he lowers the price. Conversely, if bad weather has reduced the supply of tomatoes, while the demand is constant, the greengrocer will put up the price, reckoning that the public will continue to buy his tomatoes at the higher figure; some will be put off by the higher price, but since supply is less than normal demand, a somewhat decreased demand will still buy up all the tomatoes available. But the general truth of the law of supply and demand does not mean that *every* variation in supply or demand will have a definite effect on prices. There is usually a time lag before a change in supply or demand is sufficiently prominent to affect prices. Again, sometimes a glut in production will lead producers to destroy part of the crop instead of lowering their prices to the degree necessary to sell it all.

Here is another example, slightly more sophisticated. Lord Keynes's book, *The General Theory of Employment, Interest and Money* (1936), is commonly held to have been a landmark in the history of economics and to have given the subject a new direction. In the first part of that book, Keynes argued that the classical theory about the relation of wages to employment was mistaken. He put forward a new theory and said, among other things, that his new theory depended on a 'fundamental psychological law' that when real income increases, consumption increases, but *not to the same extent*. He wrote that we can confidently accept this law 'from our knowledge of human nature and from the detailed facts of experience'.[2] Most of us can indeed call upon our own experience, or the experience of our parents, for confirmatory evidence of Keynes's generalization. But although Keynes called his generalization a 'psychological law', he cannot have supposed that it applies in *every* case. For most of us also know from experience that there are people who, at least sometimes, will spend up to the limit of their income and who, if they get an extra £5 per week in their wages, will at once go and spend the whole of it. Nevertheless such occasional exceptions do not refute Keynes's so-called 'law'; for, despite his use of the word 'law', he meant it as a *tendency*, what happens in the vast majority of cases.

In social sciences other than economics there is not much talk of 'laws'. The term is occasionally used in sociology. For example, the German sociologist Robert Michels[3] proposed an 'iron law of oligarchy', which says that any organization, even if at first democratic, will turn into an oligarchy, i.e. will be run by a few people. This seems plausible enough as a generalization but it is certainly not true universally. In an Israeli kibbutz every decision of any consequence is taken at a meeting of all the members, after discussion and by democratic vote. Much the same is true of a branch of the Society of Friends (the Quakers). A sociologist might

[2] Chap. 8. iii (Royal Economic Society edition, 1973, p. 96).
[3] *Political Parties* (1915; original German version, 1911), vi.2.

say that these examples do not matter much for sociological purposes because they concern small groups and are exceptional. Nevertheless the examples show that Michels's generalization is not rigidly true of every organization, as the term 'iron law' implies.

All so-called laws in the social sciences refer to behaviour. Most proposed laws of human behaviour can be refuted, as *laws*, simply by someone's *deciding* to do so. Take Keynes's law that a rise in real wages leads to a rise in consumption but not to the same extent. Suppose that in the present year I find that my earnings show a real increase over the past year. An increase in salary to cope with inflation would not be an increase in real income, but let us suppose that there has been an exceptional rise in the sales of my last book, bringing me a substantial amount in royalties. In the ordinary way I might well decide (confirming Keynes's generalization) to spend half the money on a special holiday and to save the rest. But now suppose that somebody says to me: 'You are *bound* to spend part, but not all, of that extra money. It is a fundamental psychological *law*.' I could easily decide to act differently. 'Nonsense!' I might say. 'In order to prove that there is no such binding law, I shall spend the whole of the extra money, or I shall save the whole of it, just this once.' There are occasions when I would not be able to take a decision contrary to my usual tendency. For instance, suppose I were told that a person with my constitution and personal history is incapable of committing a murder; I do not claim that I could deliberately falsify that prediction. But with most so-called laws of social science it is perfectly possible to go against the usual tendency – for once or twice.

It may be said that a deliberate decision to refute a law of behaviour is not really an exception to the law because a further causal factor has been introduced, namely the desire to refute the original law; the action that now takes place will fall under a different, more complex, law which takes account of such a desire. But this objection begs the question and misses the point. It begs the question because it assumes that a causal factor must be interpreted in terms of necessary, universal law. And it misses the point because the purpose of the argument is to support the contention that so-called laws in the social sciences are not in fact *universal* regularities; they are tendencies. The argument is that whatever generalization is put forward as a universal regularity can (usually) be shown to lack universality.

You can have a perfectly sound science which deals in tendencies, not laws; for you can predict with probability from a tendency, and that is quite good enough for many purposes. Think, for example, of an insurance company which uses the statistics of burglaries or accidents or deaths to compute premiums for its policies. Provided that these statistics show a regular trend, they can be used by the company's actuary as reliable evidence of probable statistics for the future. The regularity of the relevant occurrences is nearly always less than 100 per cent, but that does not make the actuary's work unscientific.

It seems to me, therefore, that the actual facts and procedures of the social sciences do not lend support to the case for determinism. Causal explanation in the social sciences is not a matter of bringing events under universal or necessary laws, as it generally is in the physical sciences. This does not prove that it is a mistake to think of human actions as necessitated, and you may want to ask what does causation mean, in the case of actions, if it does not mean necessitation. To that question I shall return in Chapter 10. However, our discussion has shown that the determinist is mistaken in thinking that his interpretation of the causal axiom ('Every event has a cause' implies 'Every event is necessitated') is borne out by the character of causal explanation in the sciences.

The second argument for determinism needs less discussion than the first. The second argument is that it is often possible to predict a person's future actions from a knowledge of things like his character, individual history, and social conditions. Such predictions are usually made with probability, not certainty, and this accords with what I have been saying about explanation in the social sciences in terms of trends or tendencies. It is highly probable that Jack Robinson, or anyone else, will conform to Keynes's generalization about spending habits in relation to a rise in real income. It is highly probable that Jack Robinson, in the light of his personal history, will use the extra money for house-improvement rather than for a holiday. But predictions with a high probability do not imply necessity.

Some predictions of behaviour go beyond probability. If a child is still not walking at the age of eighteen months but shows no symptoms of muscular or other relevant deficiency, a doctor may well feel able to assure the parents that the child will quite certainly be walking before his second birthday. Again, a psychiatrist may feel able to say that a kleptomaniac, let loose in a store with no supervision, will quite certainly succumb to the temptation to steal. The doctor and the psychiatrist will no doubt tell us that the evidence on which they are relying contains no exceptions, it is evidence of 100 per cent regularity. If so, I for one would see no reason to query the assumption of determinism in these instances. So far as the child is concerned, nobody would suggest that learning to walk has anything to do with deliberate choice. Kleptomaniacs are different. In the absence of expert psychological knowledge, common-sense opinion would tend to be sceptical of the claim that a thief, if not actually insane, had no choice. It is reasonable to revise that opinion when presented with solid evidence. It is also reasonable to suppose that further revisions of commonsense opinion are likely to be called for in the future when scientific investigation discovers universal regularities in behaviour associated with other types of psychological abnormality. But it is not at all reasonable to attribute necessity to a regularity which is observed to have exceptions. Necessity implies universality; if behaviour of a particular type *must* happen, then it will happen in every case. If there are exceptions, we have a tendency, not a necessity. When predictions of behaviour can be made with probability but not certainty, because the relevant evidence includes some exceptions, there is no warrant for inferring that the behaviour is necessitated.

You may ask: where does the probability come from, then, if not from a necessity in the facts? Its immediate source is the (non-universal) regularity in the facts, but then we want to know whether the regularity is not due to some underlying necessity. A common source of regularity in behaviour is constancy of psychological traits, whether they be innate desires or acquired habits. The causal influence of such psychological traits is not in question. What is in question is whether that causal influence has the character of necessity. Habit at any rate does not seem to have that character. One can make a habit and one can break a habit. An important difference between habit and addiction is that a habit can be broken, with some effort but without calling upon an outside agency, by the person who is subject to it. As we say, you can break a habit by will-power. In other words, you can, with an effort, choose not to follow the habitual path, and in time, after repeated efforts, the habit loses its strength. According to our ordinary ways of thinking, the same thing is possible sometimes (not by any means always) with innate desires. One can to some degree resist the force of desires. The determinist will tell us that the so-called effort of will is really an opposing desire, which turns out to be the stronger of the two; but it is clear by now that he has no sound reason for interpreting the workings of the mind with a model drawn from mechanics.

Not all regularity of behaviour is the result of inborn or acquired psychological traits. Some of it is due to deliberate resolution. If a man resolves to go for a walk regularly at the weekend, and if he is not a feeble character whose resolutions count for nothing, he is likely to take a walk on most weekends, though not necessarily on all. Practical resolution is itself the exercise of choice. Our weekend walker, by following up his resolution a number of times, may turn his walking into a habit. Or alternatively he may continue the regular pattern of his behaviour simply because he consciously follows a rational plan. Choice can make habit, choice can break habit, and choice can follow out a consistent plan. The result is regularity of behaviour, in which choice plays a causal role, but there is no reason to say that it involves necessity.

The regularities of human behaviour which allow the development of social or behavioural sciences are not incompatible with a limited area of free choice. On the contrary, the rational exercise of choice in the form of following a policy or plan is itself responsible for regular patterns of behaviour. Regularity which is not universal carries no implication of necessity. I may be mistaken in suggesting that there are no universal regularities, no strict laws, in the findings of the social sciences, and I have agreed that some human behaviour (such as that of the kleptomaniac) may display a universal regularity which precludes free will. But it is clear that most of the regularities of the social sciences are not universal. There is no good reason to suppose that these sciences are defective on that account or that they ought to, and one day will, follow the model of the physical sciences. My conclusion is therefore that the apparent conflict between the presuppositions of ethics and the presuppositions of science is not a genuine conflict.

10 Concepts of practice

Neither of the two arguments for determinism succeeds in making a sound case. Do the positive arguments for free will fare any better? Here again there are two arguments to be considered. The first is that we are conscious of free choice in our personal experience. The second is that certain concepts of morality, especially the concept of moral obligation, imply freedom of choice.

The argument from personal experience is not convincing because it is so easy for the subjective interpretation of experience to be mistaken. How often do we find that the onlooker sees more of the game, that an experienced observer can know more about the causal conditions of action than the agent himself. This is obviously true of the behaviour of children. A mother often knows, from past observation, that her child's action (perhaps a refusal to go to bed) is the effect of being overtired, while the child himself thinks that tiredness has nothing to do with it, that indeed he is not tired. The parent knows better than the child what makes him act as he does, the doctor knows better than the patient, the experienced mountaineer knows better than the novice. Sometimes the agent himself is led by later experience to see that his interpretation at the time of action was mistaken because based on limited knowledge. The seventeenth-century philosopher, Benedict Spinoza, puts the objection caustically:

The infant believes that it is by free will that it seeks the breast; the angry boy believes that by free will he wishes vengeance; the timid man thinks it is with free will he seeks flight; the drunkard believes that by a free command of his mind he speaks the things which when sober he wishes he had left unsaid.... When we dream that we speak, we believe that we do so from a free decree of the mind ... Those who believe that they speak, or are silent, or do anything else from a free decree of the mind, dream with their eyes open (*Ethics*, III. ii, schol.; translation by White and Stirling).

This is an exaggeration. The infant at the breast has not got to the stage of beliefs about free will or anything else. A man who is awake and sober can exercise a critical consciousness which he knows he could not exercise if he were dreaming or drunk. It is true, however, that the subjective interpretation of experience is liable to attribute free choice to a wider range of actions than an observer would.

There is also the puzzling fact that we cannot see where to draw a line between actions that are freely chosen and those that are not. As I said in Chapter 8, this difficulty does not justify us in inferring that there is no difference between the two ends of a spectrum, between behaviour (that of the drug addict, for instance) which is clearly felt to be compulsive and actions (such as choosing tea or coffee for breakfast) in which we do not seem in the least to be passively subject to determining forces. All the same, one is bound to be uneasy about intermediate cases. How does it feel to be tempted to steal when you are suffering from kleptomania or starvation, or for that matter when you are a youngster in conditions of social deprivation? Does the subjective experience of such people report that they can choose between stealing and not stealing? What about the subjective experience of the habitual smoker? If he is addicted to smoking, he will often feel that he *must* smoke. If he is less far gone in the habit, will he describe his subjective experience, his conscious feelings, as allowing him to choose whether or not to smoke? Sometimes yes and sometimes no? All this seems a shaky foundation on which to build a solid argument.

The second argument for free will requires more attention. It is that a central aspect of moral thought presupposes the existence of free choice. The argument usually fastens upon the concept of moral obligation: to say that someone ought, has a moral obligation, to do a certain action implies both that he can do it and that he need not do it; he has a choice. It would make no sense to tell someone that he ought to do something if you thought that it was not open to him to do it, or if you thought that he would necessarily do it anyway. Again, if you say, of something done in the past, that you (or someone else) ought not have done it, you imply that there was a choice; an alternative action could have been done instead.

The presupposition applies not only to the concept of obligation but also to others which are connected with obligation. The ideas of moral responsibility, moral guilt, and remorse all presuppose the existence of free choice. This is not always true of responsibility. If one has caused some damage unintentionally (e.g. stood on a neighbour's toes in a crush or accidentally broken his window with a cricket ball), one feels a sense of responsibility calling for an apology and a readiness to make up for the damage if this can be done. But if one has done some harm deliberately and intentionally, then one is responsible to a greater degree – not only liable to make up for the harm, as being the cause of it, but culpable for a moral fault. That is to say, moral responsibility will then include moral guilt. (Legal guilt does not always have this character; some legal offences carry 'strict liability', i.e. are held to have been committed whenever the law is in fact broken even if there was no intention to break it.) This fuller idea of moral responsibility, and its included idea of moral guilt, presuppose that a deliberate act is a freely chosen act and could have been avoided. A charge of moral culpability can be rebutted with the claim that one could not help doing what one did. If the action could not have been avoided, then one is not culpable. Culpability implies that one could have acted differently. The same thing is true of remorse. If one has harmed another unintentionally, it is proper to think and speak of regret, but it does not make sense to employ the idea of remorse. The difference corresponds to the difference between the weaker and the stronger meanings of responsibility. The idea of remorse is apt only where a person has done wrong deliberately and could have chosen to act otherwise.

Along with these ideas goes that of just punishment. We do talk of 'punishing' a dog for doing what it has been trained not to do, but the word is not then used in its full sense. Punishment presupposes guilt and, as we have just seen, the idea of moral guilt presupposes freedom of choice. This is why there is reluctance to use the term 'punishment' in the law for offences of strict liability. If you have unwittingly parked your car in a place where parking is not permitted, you have committed an offence and are liable to a 'penalty', but neither the magistrates nor the police would want to call it a 'punishment'.

The implications of ordinary usage are not altogether clear on these matters, however, and a determinist may say that they are confused and untrustworthy. Take first the idea of obligation. Outside the context of ethics the terms 'ought' and 'obliged' are sometimes used without any implication of free choice. We may say of a train that it ought to reach its destination in ten minutes, meaning that it will do so if it conforms to the scheduled time of arrival, or else that it will do so if it continues its present speed of sixty miles per hour for the ten miles which remain to be covered. The word 'ought' here refers to a logical necessity. Again, we can use the word 'obliged' to refer to a factual necessity, when, for example, we say that the driver of a car was obliged to make a detour because part of the direct route was blocked. The moral and the prudential uses of the words 'ought' and 'obliged' certainly do refer to a kind of necessity, the binding character of a moral or prudential principle. This analogy between moral and prudential obligation on the one hand and logical and factual necessity on the other is the reason why the same terms, 'ought' and 'obliged', can be used in all four types of context.

Strictly speaking, however, only factual necessity is a genuine necessity in the sense of precluding any alternative from taking place. When the car driver's usual route is blocked, he literally cannot drive his car along it. But the train which is due to reach its destination in ten minutes can be late; and the man who, as a matter of ethics or prudence, ought to catch an early train can fail to do so. In itself this does not imply freedom of choice. The train which is late does not choose to be late, and usually its driver has not chosen to be late either. Many libertarians think that prudential obligation, unlike moral, does not presuppose freedom of choice, because prudential action is motivated by the desire for one's own best interests and because these philosophers accept the determinist case for actions motivated by desire. The different uses of the idea of obligation show that it is usually not identical with a literal idea of necessity but also that it need not imply freedom of choice. You have to look at the context and not just at the word. When someone says that the train ought to arrive at its destination in ten minutes, it is clear that his use of the word 'ought' expresses the conclusion of an inference and has nothing to do with prescription. But when he says that you ought to catch an early train, it is plain that the word 'ought' then does have a prescriptive force. This is true both of moral and of prudential obligation, and for my part I cannot see any good reason to distinguish between them in regard to their presupposition of free will. When the doctor says that you ought to take more exercise, he implies that you have a choice between following his advice and not doing so.

The determinist also points to ambiguities in the ideas of responsibility, guilt, and punishment. I have noted that these terms are used in a weaker and a stronger sense, the weaker carrying no implication of free choice. This leads the determinist to maintain that the stronger sense too can be understood in a way consistent with determinism. Deliberate wrongdoing has its cause in a decision by the agent. That decision is itself caused, e.g. by a desire for gain or a feeling of anger or spite. According to the determinist, the point of having the stronger sense of responsibility, guilt, and punishment is to modify the causal conditions of decision in the future. The threat of punishment adds the causal factor of fear to counteract the causal factor which has produced the harmful act. A feeling of moral guilt, and the stronger sense of responsibility which includes a feeling of moral guilt, can have the same sort of effect as the fear of punishment. They too can help to counteract the desire or emotion which caused the harmful act. A similar explanation can be given of the distinction between regret and remorse; a feeling of regret produces an apology, while a feeling of remorse acts as a motivating force for the future. All these things can be accommodated within a deterministic scheme of interpretation.

Paradox is sometimes the most effective method of making a philosophical point. A lively picture of the deterministic interpretation can be found in Samuel Butler's satirical novel, *Erewhon*. Butler describes a utopia in which, among other things, public attitudes towards sickness and crime are transposed. Illness is regarded as a shocking fall from grace. People who have caught a cold receive a sharp lecture from a judge on the wickedness of their ways and are sentenced to imprisonment or a fine. If anybody visits them during the period of their sentence, he will treat their illness as something shameful; and after they have recovered, they will hope that as few people as possible will get to know about this shady episode in their past. On the other hand, crime is treated as a mishap calling for sympathy. People who have committed a theft or an assault receive the commiseration of their friends. They are visited by a 'straightener', who inquires into all the symptoms and then prescribes a remedy. The remedy is often an unpleasant one – a restricted diet, perhaps, or even being regularly flogged – but then, as we know, remedies for natural disorders often have to be unpleasant, and it is worth putting up with them in order to get better. Once he has recovered, the erstwhile criminal will often receive kindly inquiries about his moral character and expressions of hope that he is now fully cured.

Butler writes as if illness were voluntary and crime involuntary, but of course he does not mean the first seriously. He wants us to regard crime as involuntary, as a form of illness; he wants punishment to be replaced by treatment. This need not be something less unpleasant; isolation or flogging may be the best way to reduce crime. But what should be changed, Butler thinks, is the attitude. Condemnation should be replaced by a caring concern. Penal measures are a social necessity. We should recognize, however, that the anti-social actions which they are designed to prevent are themselves the result of psychological necessity.

Butler believes that our present concepts of responsibility, guilt, and punishment are mistaken and need to be scrapped. Some determinists, however, write as if their account of these things were giving a correct interpretation of the actual thought and practice of everyday life. They claim that the libertarian misunderstands ethical thought. After all, they say, ethical thought takes it for granted that moral exhortation and reprobation, the incentive of praise and reward, the disincentive of blame and punishment, can have an effect on future action. It assumes that character affects conduct, that education affects character. The libertarian, they suppose, denies these causal links; he must be maintaining that freely chosen action takes place by chance.

Whatever be the correct interpretation of ethical thought, this kind of determinist is certainly wrong in what he says about libertarianism. Free choice is not chance. It means an absence of necessitation but not an absence of causation. The libertarian allows that conduct is causally influenced by character and that character is causally influenced by education, moral exhortation, and other things too. The determinist supposes that causation must be a matter of necessitation and that therefore a denial of necessitation is a denial of any causal link at all.

Well, if causation does not mean necessitation, what does it mean? The idea of a causal law, on which the determinist relies, is a relatively modern concept. When Aristotle analysed the notion of causation he distinguished four elements or 'four causes', none of which involved the idea of causal law. Aristotle's four causes were formal, material, efficient, and 'final' (or teleological). The fourth is called the final or teleological cause because the Latin word for an end or purpose is *finis*, while the Greek word is *telos*. Aristotle meant that in the production of something there must be (*a*) a form which is imposed (*b*) on matter (*c*) by an agency (*d*) for some end or purpose. For example, if a sculptor makes a statue, a form or shape is imposed on a lump of stone by the sculptor in order to glorify a god or please a patron. Aristotle applied his analysis also to natural processes such as generation but he acquired it in the first instance from thinking about artificial production such as the work of the sculptor. Of his four causes, the one that is relevant to our discussion is efficient cause. When Aristotle said that the sculptor is the efficient cause of the statue, he did not suppose that there is any question of necessity about it. The sculptor is a human agent, he acts upon the stone and changes its shape. He produces the statue, he causes the stone to acquire a specific form. There is no reason why we should think of this as a matter of necessity. In the ordinary way we should regard the sculptor as exercising the free creativity of an artist; he chooses to chip the stone this way and that in order to produce the shape he is after. This is clearly a process of causation, of making, and it does not cease to be a process of causation when we think of it as a series of free choices.

In physical science, as we have seen, the idea of causation is associated with necessary laws. But this is not true of the idea of causation employed in all disciplines. Consider first the idea of causation in history.

When a historian inquires into the cause (or causes) of some important event, he does not look for a necessary law, of which this event is an instance. Suppose, for example, he asks why Julius Caesar took the fateful decision in 49 BC to cross the Rubicon and march on Rome, initiating the events which put an end to the Republic. The historian will seek evidence of Caesar's fears of impeachment, his sense of what was in justice due to him for his military achievements, his ambition, his feelings about his rivals. In all this the historian and his readers will rely upon an awareness of general psychological tendencies – how people generally are moved by fear, ambition, and the rest. But all the time the historian and his readers will also be aware that they are thinking about an exceptional character. An ordinary man, if faced with the conflicting thoughts and emotions which faced Caesar, would not have had the daring to do what Caesar did. And it would be foolish to suggest that the historian thinks of Caesar's decision as an instance of how all daring men behave in such circumstances. The circumstances were exceptional and the man was exceptional. The historian makes use of generalizations but the answer to his own causal inquiry is pre-eminently individual.

Often the historian's question will concern a broader, a more amorphous, event than the decision of one individual. He may, for example, inquire into the causes of the French Revolution or the causes of the Second World War. The event to be explained here is a complex one, consisting of the actions of a number of people over a period of time. Yet here again the historian's explanation will be tied to France in the years leading up to 1789, or to Europe in the years leading up to 1939. The explanation will not take the form of trying to bring the complex event under a universal law: e.g. that whenever the social divisions in a country produce a certain degree of misery and resentment, the masses will revolt; or that whenever a proud nation is subjected to humiliating restrictions after being conquered in a war, it will set out to be itself the conqueror in a new war. Some kinds of sociological theory (Marxist theory, for example) suggest recurrent patterns or 'laws' of historical change. Whether or not they are worthy of serious consideration as one type of history, they are not typical of historical explanation and they are too general to afford satisfactory answers to the vast majority of questions about causation in history.

I have mentioned the attempt in some kinds of sociological theory to produce a quasi-scientific schema of causal laws to account for changes in the history of society. As with other so-called laws of sociology, such generalizations cannot sustain a claim to be universal (a point already dealt with in Chapter 9). It is worth noting, however, that sociology also makes use of other types of causal explanation, different both from the notion of causation used in physical science and from that used in history.

One type is functional explanation. A sociologist or social anthropologist may want to explain why a particular society retains an unusual social institution (i.e. a pattern of behaviour which is generally accepted and followed). Take, for example, the caste system of India and Sri Lanka. It may have arisen originally as the result of conquest, the invading conquerors giving themselves a superior social status to that of the conquered. The question of origins is a matter for historical inquiry. But there is the further question why the caste system has persisted. The caste system is peculiar in its rigidity; it does not allow for the crossing of social barriers by some individuals, as is possible in other systems of social stratification. Why has this peculiar system persisted in India for so long? The answer offered is that the system serves a social function in enabling groups with different cultural backgrounds to live in the same society without conflict. The suggestion is that the rigid separation of the castes, in the socially intimate matters of marriage and taking meals together, avoids the tension which arises when there is intermarriage between different cultural groups. The cause of the persistence of the institution is the supposedly useful role it plays as an element in the social structure as a whole. This idea of causation has nothing necessary or universal about it. My example of the caste system shows that the concept can be applied to a phenomenon which is very unusual among societies. Understanding comes from seeing the relationship of the institution to the particular social structure as a whole, not from seeing it as an instance of a universal (or even a general) rule.

Yet another concept of causation in sociology is 'cumulative causation', first enunciated by Gunnar Myrdal in his book, *An American Dilemma* (1944), a pioneering work about the position of blacks in the United States. Myrdal pointed out that poor conditions among blacks and prejudice among whites were liable to reinforce each other; there was a cumulative process of reciprocal causation. Ignorance and limited performance on the part of blacks appeared to whites to confirm their opinion of black inferiority, while that opinion itself helped to block the opportunities for blacks to improve their position. The idea of cumulative causation has since been applied to other social problems. For the purposes of sociology it is a valid and valuable concept of causation. It describes a real process. But it does not carry with it any idea of necessity. On the contrary, Myrdal also pointed out that the direction of the cumulative circular movement can be reversed. If governmental intervention provides greater educational opportunity for blacks, some at least will be able to show that they can acquire knowledge and skill; this in turn will help to reduce some of the white prejudice based on the assumption that blacks are inevitably ignorant and incompetent; the reduction of prejudice in its turn will help to reduce further the barriers to opportunities for blacks; and so on. The reciprocal process of cumulative causation will now work towards a gradual improvement on both sides, in place of the previous movement of a gradually worsening situation on both sides. The change is the result of an additional causal factor, the governmental intervention, but the point is that neither the process of cumulative causation nor the simple causal factor of governmental action is thought of as an instance of a universal necessary law. The additional causal factor of action by the government is treated as the opposite of necessary; it is a choice which the government can, but does not have to, make.

This last point brings out another important feature of causal inquiries in some disciplines. Myrdal's investigation was designed not only to explain but also to propose remedies; it was a practical inquiry. There are disciplines of practical inquiry in which the very concept of cause has a practical or prescriptive dimension. The purpose of an inquiry by a team of engineers into the cause of a traffic accident is intended to find out what went 'wrong', what happened which 'ought not' to have happened, and what *should be done* to prevent a similar thing happening again. Suppose that a certain bend in a trunk road is a black spot for accidents. The inquiry tries to discover 'the cause' of the frequency of accidents. It might conclude that 'the cause' is that the camber of the road is too steep for this bend in wet weather; or that 'the cause' is excessive speed by motorists. If the idea of causation were being used without a practical intention, one might say that the camber of the road or the speed of the cars using it was only one of several factors making up the totality of causal conditions. For example, if (as the first answer suggested) the accidents all occur in wet weather, then rain, or a wet surface, is a necessary part of the total causal conditions. But the engineers would think they had failed to do their job if they had said that rain was the cause of the accidents. When they talk of 'the cause', they are looking for something which can be *remedied* by human action. Their business is to prevent the recurrence of the accidents. They can advise the transport authority to alter the camber of the road or to put up a notice restricting the speed of vehicles at that point. They cannot change the weather. So the notion of 'cause', as used in such inquiries, includes a practical or prescriptive meaning: to ask what is 'the cause' of the accidents is, in part, to ask what should be done in order to prevent a recurrence of the accidents.[1]

A different, but related, practical use of the concept can be found in the law. Civil law cases about an accident are similarly often concerned with inquiry into the cause of the accident. Here again a particular action or event which is pinpointed as 'the cause' is only one of several factors making up the total causal conditions of the unfortunate event which occurred. What the court wants to determine is who, if anyone, should be made *liable* for the damage which has occurred.[2] Is anyone to blame?

[1] Cf. R.G. Collingwood, *An Essay on Metaphysics* (1940), chap. 31.
[2] Cf. Lord Wright, 'Notes on Causation and Responsibility in English Law', *Cambridge Law Journal*, Nov. 1955.

Has someone been negligent in failing to do what a reasonable man can be expected to do? If so, he is required to meet the cost of the damage. If not, the person who has suffered the damage, or his insurance company, has to put up with bearing the loss without recompense. The court may decide that there was some negligence on both sides and that the action of the person who suffered the damage was a part of the cause. The court's decision could as well be expressed in terms of responsibility, and when it says that the action of a person was a part-cause it is assigning part of the responsibility.

While the engineering inquiry is intended to find out what should be done to prevent similar accidents in the future, the legal inquiry is intended to decide who should be required to pay for the damage done in the past. Both are practical inquiries concerned with prescription. Their findings of 'the cause' of an event have nothing to do with setting out a universal law of necessitation.

Ethics, like engineering and the law, employs a practical mode of thought. It assumes that alternative options are often open to us. Freedom of choice is a presupposition of moral thought and language. This, of course, is no guarantee of the truth of a belief in free will. Our customary ideas in ethics and in other modes of practical thought might be mistaken. If there really were a pervasive conflict between a libertarian presupposition of practical thought and a determinist presupposition of theoretical understanding, there would indeed be ground for suspicion. It might be suggested that, while prescription has its own value, explanation is what gives us truth. We have, however, seen that determinism is not presupposed by all explanation. In particular, determinism is not presupposed by the types of explanation found in history and the social sciences, the disciplines which seek to understand human action.

Ethics and evolution

11 The relevance of Darwinism

If one talks to scientists about moral philosophy, they often ask about the relevance of evolution to ethics. An examination of suggestions that have been made can help to clarify ideas and may even make some genuine headway in the criticism of common assumptions. The theory of evolution has been connected with ethics in two different ways. The first suggestion is that ethics is a product of evolution. There is little or no dispute about the general truth of this suggestion, though details of the process of the evolution of ethics are still speculative. The second suggestion is that evolution can provide a practical guide for ethics, and this is very much a matter of dispute.

The first suggestion is that our moral capacities ('conscience') and our moral ideas have evolved by a process which is part of the general process of evolution or at least analogous to the general process of evolution. By 'conscience' is meant the capacity of human beings to make moral judgements which can then motivate action.

What does it mean to say that our moral capacities and ideas have evolved? Sometimes 'evolved' is just a synonym for 'developed'. In that event the term 'evolution' has little or no explanatory value. Charles Darwin's theory of evolution had explanatory force because it showed how all the different species of living things can be correlated together in a *single* process of development, in which an enormous diversity of results can all be put down to a single set of causes, namely, the survival of some varieties, through a process of natural 'selection', in 'the struggle for existence' between forms of life, all of which reproduce themselves in far greater numbers than can be nourished by the environment. Darwin used the word 'selection' metaphorically, to show how a natural process can appear to resemble choice or design. The natural process does not include any deliberate picking out of some varieties for survival; they survive because they happen to be better fitted to do so than their rivals. But the result is similar to the effect of deliberate selection in artificial processes, as when a gardener selects one plant for survival and throws away its neighbours that would otherwise compete with it for sustenance. Darwin's theory had great explanatory force because it substituted the simple hypothesis of a single process for the alternative hypothesis of a special creation for each of the many different species of plants and animals.

A theory of the evolution of ethics will have similar explanatory force if it can show that the development of conscience and of ethical ideas is a part of the same process of evolution by natural selection which explains the origin of biological species. It will have less, but still some, explanatory force if it takes the more limited form of showing that conscience, instead of being a 'separate creation', has developed from other human endowments responding and adapting to the stimuli of natural and social environment. A theory of the first type was put forward by Darwin in *The Descent of Man*, where he tried to show how the intellectual and moral capacities of man could have owed their development, at least partly, to the process of natural selection. Modern psychologists do not try to use natural selection as the medium whereby the moral capacities have developed. They have instead constructed theories of the second type, showing how conscience is built up from other mental endowments, such as love and fear, responding to the stimuli of family and wider social environment. Sociologists and anthropologists have provided similar evidence of changing environmental stimuli to account for changes in moral ideas, in *what* is approved and disapproved by conscience as right and wrong, just and unjust, and so on.

The evolution of ethics as portrayed by modern psychologists and social scientists, therefore, has little in common with the specifically Darwinian concept of evolution through natural selection. The type of evolutionary explanation they give follows lines laid down before Darwin. This is particularly true of accounts of the development of the moral capacities. Darwin himself knew something of the views of contemporary and earlier philosophers about the development of conscience from social impulses and especially from sympathy. He drew largely on the work of Alexander Bain, but he knew that the idea originated with Hume and Adam Smith in the eighteenth century.

Like every genius, Darwin built upon the work of his predecessors. The idea of a struggle for existence was taken from the theory of the economist and demographer, Thomas Malthus, about the growth of human population. To note Darwin's debt to Malthus is not to disparage his own achievement. The originality of genius lies not so much in thinking of an idea as in seeing how to make the best use of it. Malthus had held that population tends to increase faster than the means of subsistence but is restrained by the 'positive checks' of famine, war, and disease, and by the 'preventive checks' of 'moral restraint' and 'vice'. His theory thus allows a distinction between natural tendencies that cause a lot of people to be born and then killed off, and premeditated measures to prevent them being born. Darwin followed out the implications of the natural causes in the absence of preventive measures, and used this situation as a hypothesis to account not merely for the numbers of animals and plants but also for the extinction or survival of their different varieties. His ability to use the theory in this way depended in part on his powers of analysis, but more on the stimulus to those powers provided by his astonishingly wide and careful observation of similarities and differences in the data of biology. Although Darwin's theory was, as he himself observed, an 'application' of Malthus, it was none the less an epoch-making discovery.

It is quite otherwise with Darwin's borrowings from Adam Smith and Bain on the development of the moral capacities, and Darwin would not have claimed any special originality here. When he came to discuss this topic in *The Descent of Man*, his purpose was not to provide a new theory but simply to show that the peculiar endowments of man were no objection to the evolution of man from another form of animal life. He paid special attention to the moral capacities because, he said, conscience is the most important difference between man and the lower animals.

He did, however, add something to previous theories of the development of conscience from sympathy and other impulses. The previous theories had confined themselves to man. They showed how conscience develops from feelings and desires with which all normal human beings are naturally endowed, modified by reaction to the attitudes of their fellows in social intercourse. To this Darwin added three things, all due to his biological interests.[1]

(a) In the first place he suggested that the initial social impulses which form the basis of conscience are to be found in animals also. In particular, he described some interesting examples of animal behaviour which he thought could only be motivated by sympathy. (b) Secondly, he suggested that natural selection is likely to have been an important causal factor in the development of 'social instincts'. An individual with strong social instincts would be *less* likely to survive than a selfish individual intent on saving his own skin, and therefore would be less likely to leave offspring inheriting his instincts. But because his type of behaviour is more conducive to the welfare of the group, he would, as Hume had said, be praised by his fellows, and the praise of his qualities would cause others to emulate it and to counsel emulation in the teaching of their own young. To this Darwin added that an increase of such qualities in a group by the force of example would give that group a greater survival-value

[1] *The Descent of Man*, 2nd edition (1874), chap. 4.

than would be possessed by a group whose members acted only for their individual welfare. (*c*) Finally, Darwin was inclined to believe that the qualities of mind and behaviour acquired through example and education were transmitted by heredity to offspring.

Darwin's evidence for sympathetic behaviour in non-human animals is mainly anecdotal and would not satisfy modern standards of scientific reliability. It can, however, now be supported by convincing evidence from controlled scientific experiments. An example is given by Professor James Rachels in a book about the moral implications of Darwinism.[2] A group of rhesus monkeys were trained to obtain food by pulling a chain when a light showed. They were then enabled to learn that their pulling one such chain also resulted in a severe painful shock (produced by an electrical charge) for another monkey whom they could see through a one-way mirror, while pulling a different chain did not. Before they had grasped that pain for the other monkey occurred only when they pulled the first chain, a clear majority of them deliberately refrained from operating the device, although this meant that they went without food, in some cases for several days.

Darwin's second point is clearly sound but he has no real evidence for linking it, in his third point, with heredity. The idea that the *acquired* qualities of parents would be inherited by their children is one among several traces in Darwin of Lamarck's theory of evolution, which came to be discredited by Darwin's theory of natural selection. But in fact Darwin's own critical spirit led him to express doubt about the Lamarckian notion even when he was inclined to accept it. If habits of behaviour are transmitted by inheritance, he said, this should apply to 'superstitious customs or senseless habits' as much as to virtues, but he knew of no evidence to support that.

James Rachels has suggested[3] that the modern science of genetics, unknown in Darwin's day, can provide an explanation of the inheritance of social instincts that is purely biological and fits in with the theory of natural selection. Darwin had reasonably assumed that the basic form of social affection is that between parents and children, and while he had no idea just how this might be a result of natural selection, he inferred, from the general success of his theory, that natural selection must be 'to a large extent' the cause of parental and filial affection. Rachels thinks that the link lies in the inheritance of genes. He suggests that family affection is to be explained in the same way as family resemblance. Children tend to resemble one of their parents (or both in different respects) and to

---

[2] *Created from Animals: The Moral Implications of Darwinism* (1990), pp. 149–52.
[3] pp. 154–8.

resemble some of their siblings, because each child inherits half of its genes from one parent and half from the other. Genes can be responsible for some traits of character as well as for physical qualities, and Rachels believes that such traits of character include altruistic affection and concern. If so, the altruistic behaviour that results from the responsible genes will favour the survival of the altruistic parents' children and therefore will favour also the survival of the responsible genes. By contrast, the children of parents who lack these genes and are neglectful will have a lesser chance of survival, as will the genes that determine neglectful behaviour towards one's young. So, in the course of time, the first set of genes will become more widespread and the latter set will tend to disappear.

This piece of reasoning is, of course, hypothetical. It will (or may) be true *if* parental affection and concern are determined by specific genes. Rachels offers one piece of empirical evidence about 'kin altruism' which, he thinks, supports the hypothesis. The evidence comes from ants. In most species of sexually reproducing animals, including man, the pattern of gene transmission is such that all progeny have, on average, about half of the same genes as any of their siblings. But with ants there is a different pattern: a female ant shares three-quarters of its genes with female siblings and one-quarter with male siblings. In an ant colony the worker ants, who supply food for the rest, are all females. A study has found that they provide about three times more food for their sisters than for their brothers; but where the workers have been 'enslaved' from another colony and so are not related by kin to those they serve, they provide roughly the same amount of food for males and females alike. The correlation, in the first group, between genes and behaviour is certainly striking (though my own reading of the paper cited by Rachels suggested that it is not quite so clear-cut). But should the behaviour be regarded as kin *altruism* or kin *favouritism*? The term 'altruism' is used by the investigators in a technical sense to mean behaviour that benefits another at some cost (such as effort) to oneself. The whole of the service provided by the worker ants is 'altruistic', irrespective of whether they are serving kin or unrelated ants. Their tendency to favour sister ants is not an increase of altruism. Since it is determined by possession of the same genes, it is analogous to an extended egoism rather than altruism. One may say the same about the special affection of parents for progeny.

The term 'kin altruism', as used by sociobiologists, simply means other-serving behaviour shown towards kin, with no necessary implication that biological kinship provides the motivating cause. Rachels goes on to discuss their consideration of animal behaviour which benefits another animal who is not related by kin. They call this 'reciprocal altruism', because it is a matter of doing a service for another animal in the expectation of receiving a similar service in return ('I'll scratch your back if you scratch mine'). Here the underlying motive is more plainly egoistic. If the 'kin altruism' of worker ants is determined by genes, their 'altruistic' behaviour towards unrelated ants is not. Nor is the 'reciprocal altruism' of other animals.

There is, of course, no reason to doubt that genetic influence on familial instincts in lower animals is repeated in man. But even if we accept that genes play a part in the affection and concern which human beings show towards kin, we know from common experience that close association has at least as great an influence. Adoptive parents usually come to feel as much affection and concern for their children as do biological parents; and if a natural mother doubts this, as she well may, on the ground that no adoptive parent can match what she feels as the result of gestation and giving birth, she is appealing to *experience*, not genetics, and what she says sets her apart from the biological father as much as from any adoptive parent. On the other side, children are liable to feel attached to whoever does most in caring for them, whether it be a biological or an adoptive parent, a nanny, or anyone else. One may come, through close association, to feel as warm an affection and concern for friends or colleagues as for siblings and cousins, to say nothing of the rivalry or jealousy that can counteract affection for brothers and sisters.

In his account of the development of the moral capacities, Darwin saw that there is a problem in explaining why the promptings of conscience are given *precedence* over self-regarding motives. It cannot be because they are stronger, for everyone knows that in general this is untrue. Darwin's answer to the problem is that 'the social instincts are ever present and persistent' as the result of reflection. We keep on thinking of what other people think of us, imagining their approval or disapproval. By contrast, self-interested motives such as hunger or a desire for revenge are temporary and can be fully satisfied for the time being. Darwin notes that this is not true of some self-interested desires, such as the coveting of another man's property, but, he says, even here 'the satisfaction of actual possession is generally a weaker feeling than the desire'.

His solution is obviously lame, as his own qualification shows. If the desire for another man's property can be persistent, it is not made less so by the fact that the satisfaction of possession is a weaker feeling than the desire. It is easy enough to say that the desire to satisfy hunger or revenge is temporary, but it is not so easy to say this of all self-regarding motives; and the persistence of some self-regarding desires is not removed by the alleged fact that the satisfaction of them is a weaker feeling than the desires themselves.

Bishop Joseph Butler, in the eighteenth century, drew a distinction between two types of motive, which he called reflective 'principles' and 'particular passions'. Conscience is a reflective principle. Hunger and the desire for revenge are particular passions; so is pity. Butler is not clear whether there is a reflective principle of altruistic feeling, as well as the principle of conscience, but he is quite clear that there is also a reflective principle of self-regard, which co-ordinates particular passions like hunger and aims at our personal good as a whole. We reflect upon the effect of our actions on our own welfare, just as we reflect upon the way they affect other people. Our use of language confirms Butler's comparison. Darwin's problem here is to explain what Butler called the 'authority', the obligatory character, of conscience, which we express by the use of words like 'ought'. Darwin holds, as Hume and Adam Smith had held, that the obligatory character of conscience comes from reflection upon the approval and disapproval shown by our fellows. We use the word 'ought' of self-regarding actions also. To say that one ought to act in a certain way may mean that one is morally obliged, but it may equally mean that one is prudentially obliged.

If we are to give an account of the evolution of conscience, including its judgements that we ought to perform some actions and refrain from others, we must recognize that self-regard, with its judgements of 'ought' and 'ought not', is similarly a reflective and late-developed capacity. If a highly developed form of unselfishness is peculiar to man owing to his capacity for reflection, so is a highly developed form of selfishness. Darwin's omission to observe this does not weaken in the least his argument that conscience has evolved from capacities which man shares with other animals. But it is highly relevant to any contention that the direction of evolution is the direction of morality. While selfishness is directed at the good of the person concerned and does not itself aim at harm, it can in many situations have the collateral effect of harm to others. In its aim it is no more moral or immoral than its rudimentary counterpart in 'the struggle for existence'. It can be immoral at the reflective stage just because it is accompanied at that stage by the capacity for moral reflection, for thinking about the interests of others as well as of ourselves. As T. H. Huxley (a friend and stalwart champion of Darwin) said in his famous Romanes Lecture on 'Evolution and Ethics' (1893): while there is little doubt that the moral sentiments have evolved, 'the immoral sentiments have no less been evolved'.

The second suggestion about ethics and evolution, namely that a study of evolution can be a guide for ethics, has no place in the works of Darwin. But ideas which have produced striking advances in any one field of inquiry are always (and rightly) tried out in others. Often the first step comes in philosophical speculation, and Darwin's theory of evolution soon gave rise to a crop of metaphysical and moral philosophies. Nineteenth-century attempts to base ethics on evolution were forcefully criticized by T. H. Huxley. He said that people who spoke of the ethics of evolution were confusing this ridiculous idea with the sensible one of the evolution of ethics. The moral sentiments and tendencies had no doubt evolved, but so had the immoral. Evolution in itself was therefore 'incompetent to furnish any better reason why what we call good is preferable to what we call evil than we had before'. In fact, he argued, the aim of ethical endeavour goes against the cosmic process of evolution. 'Its influence is directed, not so much to the survival of the fittest, as to the fitting of as many as possible to survive.'[4]

Nobody thinks that things become better just because they are later in time, that the hangover is preferable to the party because it comes on the morning after. Why, then, should it be supposed that the direction of evolution can be a guide for ethics? One reason is that 'more evolved', unlike 'later', includes in its meaning the idea of being superior, higher on a scale of value. But now we need to ask whether the scale of value implied is the same as that used in ethics.

What criterion of value is in fact used when one organism is said to be 'higher' in the evolutionary scale than another? At first sight, it might seem that the natural results of the process of evolution supply the criterion. Natural selection results in 'the survival of the fittest', and it is easy to suppose that 'fittest' means 'best'. So indeed it does if we are thinking of what is best fitted to survive. But in that case the survival of the fittest means no more than the survival of those *most able* to survive. Perhaps that is a slight exaggeration, at least so far as ordinary language is concerned. Normally, to call something 'good' or 'best' is to express commendation of it. So to say of one thing that it is better fitted than another to do something, is to express commendation of its greater ability, as well as to say that it has the greater ability. Nevertheless, this does not necessarily imply commendation of that which it is able to do. Bill Sykes may be best fitted to crack a safe; in the *art* of safe-cracking, we take off our hats to him. But this does not mean that we take off our hats to safe-cracking in preference to leaving other people's property alone. To be sure, we do not feel the same about survival as we do about safe-cracking. Most of us do not want to crack safes but do want to survive for as long as we can; and we also sympathize with the desire of others to survive, while having no sympathy with Bill Sykes's desire to crack safes.

---

[4] Reprinted in T. H. Huxley and Julian Huxley, *Evolution and Ethics 1893–1943* (1947), pp. 80–1.

Still, it is not survival as such that suffices to induce our sympathy. We have no sympathy with the efforts of an influenza virus to survive and multiply. A late-evolved strain of virus is fitter than earlier strains which have been eliminated by natural selection; yet no doctor feels morally obliged to let it go on surviving so successfully, any more than a policeman thinks himself morally obliged to let Bill Sykes go on with the safe-cracking which he does so successfully.

Different standards of commendation are used for different purposes. So far as safe-cracking goes, Bill Sykes is at the top. So far as ethics goes, he is near the bottom. High ability at performing any function, whether this be safe-cracking, survival, or anything else, does not necessarily go along with high ethical value. The standards of ethical evaluation do not depend upon the performance of a specific function. To speak of a good man is not to commend by the same standards as those we use when we speak of a good runner or a good burglar or even a good survivor.[5]

Furthermore, superior ability at surviving does not necessarily go along with superiority in the evolutionary scale. It is not at all clear that there is a single standard of evaluation for the purpose of grading organisms as higher or lower on the scale of evolution. Darwin pointed out that different standards are used for different biological kingdoms, for animals, for fishes, and for plants; and even within any one biological kingdom different biologists may use different standards of evaluation in determining evolutionary superiority. On the whole Darwin favoured using, as a standard, increasing differentiation and specialization of function among the parts of an organism. But he noted that continuing advance in this direction does not necessarily accompany the continuing ability of a species to survive.

Superior fitness to survive, then, is no guarantee of biological 'superiority'. Nor is biological superiority any guarantee of superior ethical value. Herbert Spencer, who was the most prominent exponent of evolutionary ethics in Darwin's day, felt it necessary to argue that biological superiority implied ethical superiority *only if* it brought with it 'a surplus of agreeable feeling'. According to Spencer, an increase of life in length and breadth (by 'breadth' he meant complexity of organization) can be called good in the ethical sense if and only if human beings find life more pleasant than painful. Plainly, therefore, his standard of ethical goodness is pleasure, not length and breadth of life.

T. H. Huxley's conclusion that evolution cannot be a guide for ethics has been challenged by some more recent biologists, including Huxley's own grandson, Julian, when invited to deliver a Romanes Lecture on the

[5] Cf. p. 30 above.

same subject of 'Evolution and Ethics' fifty years later in 1943. But Julian Huxley's disagreement is more apparent than real. He does not dispute his grandfather's view that ethical progress involves combating rather than imitating the process of natural selection. He looks instead to an extended notion of evolution as a process with three phases, physical, biological, and social. Natural selection applies only to the second of these. Evolution in the extended sense, he says, discloses a process of increasing complexity which continually produces new forms of existence; and since the new forms of the latest phase include the human experiences which we value, we can conclude that the general direction of the process of evolution is from lesser (or nil) value to greater value. We can therefore, so he says, take the natural property of increased complexity as an indication of potential novelty and value.

This is a more limited claim than Huxley supposes. He has to allow that bad as well as good novelties come out of evolution, so that the proposed criterion can give us no more than a fair possibility. He also treats it as only a supplement to the basic criterion of perceiving certain human experiences to be intrinsically good (he gives the familiar examples of beauty, knowledge, love, and devotion to a cause); we have to use that perception anyway in order to judge whether a new possibility, when it emerges, is in fact good. The one positive feature of Huxley's proposal is to encourage a readiness to welcome new possibilities in social evolution. He couples this with the further point that ethics can now affect, as well as be affected by, evolution; the future course of evolution can be changed, for good or ill, by human decisions. Few people would wish to quarrel with all this. It does make reasonable connections between ethics and evolution.

A bolder attempt to revive evolutionary ethics can be found in a work by C. H. Waddington. He really does disagree with the view of T. H. Huxley. After giving some psychological and sociological evidence for the evolution of conscience and ethical ideas, he tells us why the direction of evolution should be accepted as good.

We must accept the direction of evolution as good simply because it *is* good according to any realistic definition of that concept. We defined ethical principles as actual psychological compulsions derived from the experience of the nature of society; we stated that the nature of society is such that, in general, it develops in a certain direction; then the ethical principles which mediate the motion in that direction are in fact those adopted by that society (*Science and Ethics* (1942), p. 18).

The first sentence of this quotation tells us what Waddington thinks his argument is: any realistic definition of the concept of good shows that evolution is good. But what follows the first sentence does not give us a definition of the concept of good. What follows tells us that people's ethical principles are derived from the experience of their society and express the direction in which that society is developing. Waddington calls this a definition of ethical principles, but it is in fact a causal explanation of how they are formed. A definition tells us what a concept means; a causal explanation gives us a history of how something comes into being or changes. The so-called definition is a brief statement of the evolution of the ethical principles that people hold. It purports to specify the content of the principles with the obscure phrase that they 'mediate the motion' of social development, which I suppose means that, having been caused by social development, they reflect it; but it is not at all clear why an effect should reflect the character of its cause. What *is* clear is that the direction of social evolution does not form the content of ethical principles; it is not the standard to which people refer when they ask if something is good. After all, we can intelligibly ask whether the direction in which human society is going is itself good; and some people, having raised the question, reply that it is anything but good.

Waddington is giving us an answer to the question: 'When people commend things, do they use as their standard of commendation the direction of evolution, and if so, why?' He answers the first part of the question in the affirmative, and he answers the second part by giving us a causal account of the evolution of ethical judgement. But what is needed is an answer to a different question: 'Should we use the direction of evolution as our standard of commendation, and if so, why?' It is no answer to this question to say: 'Yes, you should, and the reason why you should is that you have always done so in the past, and so has everyone else.' Consider an analogous situation outside the field of ethics. Suppose a child says to me: 'I have always believed the earth is flat, but my friend says it is round like a ball. What should I believe, and why?' It would be absurd to answer: 'You should believe it is flat because you have done so in the past.' Nor would it be much better to answer: 'You should believe it is round because other people nowadays believe that.'

Waddington has failed to distinguish two different kinds of question and the two different kinds of answer they seek. Plainly, the question 'Should we . . . ?' is different from the question 'Do we . . . ?' The first question seeks advice, the second information. In addition, the questions 'Why should we . . . ?' and 'Why do we . . . ?' use the word 'why' in different senses. The first seeks justifying reasons, the second seeks explaining causes. To ask for facts and the causes of those facts is one thing. To ask for advice and reasons for that advice is another thing.

The distinction applies not only to queries about accepting judgements of ethics or matters of practice, but also to queries about accepting judgements of factual truth, as is shown by my example of the child's question about the earth. When the child asks *why* he should believe that the earth is round, what he is after is *evidence justifying* the acceptance of that belief. He is not asking for the *causes* of the spherical shape of the earth, nor even for the causes of my and other people's acceptance of the proposition. To see that justifying evidence for a proposition is not the same as the cause of acceptance of that proposition, consider the situation when I have given the child some evidence for the proposition that the earth is round. I tell him, for instance, that an aeroplane flying in a straight line comes back to its starting point after 25,000 miles. In the light of this evidence, he decides to accept the proposition that the earth is round. Can we now say, as I think Waddington wishes to say, that the cause of the child's acceptance is the same as the evidence justifying the proposition that he now accepts? No, we cannot. The cause of the child's acceptance is *my having told him* a moment ago what some of the evidence is, and *his seeing*, also a moment ago, that the evidence justifies the proposition. The evidence for the truth of the proposition he now accepts is not the words I uttered a moment ago or the inference he made a moment ago. The evidence is what my words and his thought referred to (namely, what happens to aeroplanes flying in a straight line for 25,000 miles), and *this* is not something that took place a moment ago.

In case anyone thinks that I have misrepresented Waddington, let me add that he himself endorses my interpretation. In publishing his essay, together with the comments of other people, in book form, he included a discussion with Herbert Dingle, a philosopher of science. Dingle says he should distinguish two different questions: 'How did I make my ethical choice?' and 'How shall I make it now?' Waddington replies: 'I cannot see that there is any real distinction here' (p. 101). The distinction might perhaps have been clearer to him if the second question had been phrased as 'How am I to make it?' instead of 'How shall I make it?' The word 'shall' is ambiguous. A question put in the form 'Shall I . . . ?' may be asking for advice, or it may be inviting a prediction. There is no logical difference (relevant to our purpose) between a report of a past action, 'You did X', and a prediction of a future action, 'You will do X'. Both are used to make statements of fact. But there *is* a logical difference between these two forms of statement on the one hand and, on the other, a sentence of the form 'You are to [or 'You should' or 'You ought to'] do X'. A sentence of this form is not used to make a statement of fact but to give a piece of advice or an instruction.

Waddington thinks the answer to the question, 'What am I to do, and for what reasons?' is the same as the answer to the question, 'What will I do, and from what causes?' This is why he supposes that a causal account of how ethical judgements have come to be what they are can supply a criterion, or rational ground, for the ethical judgements we should make. But since the two questions, and the kinds of answer they seek, are of different logical types, Waddington's argument for using the direction of evolution as the criterion for ethical judgement rests on a logical confusion.

The views of James Rachels on the relations between ethics and evolution (specifically Darwin's theory) need to be taken much more seriously. He argues that evolution undermines a major element of traditional ethics, an element which he and others call speciesism, on the analogy of racism. Racism is unwarranted discrimination in favour of one's own race against others. Speciesism is unwarranted discrimination in favour of the human species against others, a readiness to treat animals in ways that we roundly condemn if perpetrated on human beings. Rachels does not suggest that the theory of evolution logically implies that we have duties to animals. After all, you could argue to the contrary that Rachels's earlier suggestion of a genetic basis for kin altruism lends support to speciesism. Rachels is a philosopher and is thoroughly familiar with the argument that 'ought' cannot be deduced from 'is'. But this, he observes, does not rule out all rational connection between evolution and ethics. He thinks that speciesism is buttressed by the idea that human beings alone have a moral 'dignity' and that this idea depends on two factual beliefs, the biblical doctrine that man was created in the image of God and the doctrine of Greek philosophy that what differentiates man from other animals is the possession of reason. Darwinism shows these two beliefs to be false: the human species has evolved from other species, and its capacity for rational thought, while greater in degree, is not different in kind from the capacity of monkeys and of many other species of animals. A realization that the two beliefs are false undermines the support which they have given to speciesism. The traditional beliefs do not necessarily imply that human beings have no duties to animals. Rachels points out, however, that this connection has been made by some leading thinkers in the history of philosophy, including St Thomas Aquinas and Kant; they are typical of a tendency and have themselves exercised a strong influence on subsequent moral thought.

This seems a fairly persuasive case, but it is not altogether convincing. The two traditional beliefs ascribe unique qualities to human beings, but that in itself does not necessarily imply a unique standing in ethics. So far as rationality is concerned, we need only recall an oft-quoted remark of Bentham about the moral status of animals: 'the question is not, Can they *reason*? nor, Can they *talk*? but, Can they *suffer*?'[6] As for biblical doctrine, St Paul does indeed dismiss duties to animals with the rhetorical

---

[6] *Introduction to the Principles of Morals and Legislation*, chap. 17.

question, 'Doth God take care for oxen?';[7] but he knows that he is
repudiating the traditional Old Testament view, which was and is that we
do have duties to animals; the doctrine that man alone bears the image of
God was not taken to imply that man alone is the object of moral duty.
The view of Aquinas continues to influence Roman Catholic doctrine,
but people who are impressed by Kant's ethical theory are not necessarily
led to accept his view that human dignity and human reason confine the
range of ethics to human beings.[8] Rachels allows that the moral standing
of most human beings does differ from that of animals in that the human
beings have both duties and rights while the animals have only rights.
(He says most human beings, not the human species as a whole, because
duties cannot be ascribed to young children or to adults who are mentally
deficient.) When the concept of human dignity is used nowadays, as for
example in the Universal Declaration of Human Rights, it refers to the
having of duties as well as rights; and while many people jib at speaking
of animal *rights* they do not deny that human beings owe duties to
animals. It would never enter their heads to think that dignity is required
for being the object of a duty.

But perhaps the mere fact that we live in a post-Darwinian age makes
us less susceptible to the views expressed by Aquinas and Kant. Certainly
the history of European attitudes on the ethics of the treatment of
animals reveals a marked insensitivity in most quarters up to the
nineteenth century. Even today many otherwise sensitive people have no
qualms about the killing of animals or rearing them in distressing
conditions. Such people, however, are often given pause when they learn
about, or see for themselves, what these things really involve. It is
knowledge of the distress caused to the animals that gives them pause.
Would it be more effective, or as effective, simply to teach them about
evolution? It might be sometimes. Rachels points out that both scientific
and newspaper reports of experiments with animals often put quotation
marks round such words as 'pain' and 'suffering', suggesting that it is not
pain as we know it. The writers are aware of evolution, but they might be
less prone to deceive themselves if they learned more.

Rachels does not deny that there is often good reason to attach more
value to a human being than to a non-human animal (and more to a horse
than to a fly), and therefore to give preference to the former if one has to
choose between them. But if we recognize that the animal does count in
the ethical scheme of things, we shall not put trivial human interests
above vital animal interests, as when rabbits are subjected to painful and

[7] 1 Cor. 9: 9.
[8] Cf. p. 58 above.

harmful experiments in order to test the safety of cosmetics. Rachels argues that clear thinking about the moral relevance of differences between species should lead also to vegetarianism and the abolition of vivisection.

His examination of the relation between evolution and ethics, then, has serious practical consequences for our treatment of animals. But that is not all. Since there is good reason to reject speciesism, he argues, we should not retain the common view that *any* human being in *any* circumstances has 'infinite worth', as is claimed by traditional ethics under the influence of theological doctrine. This conclusion affects traditional views about the ethics of suicide, euthanasia, and other contentious issues of medical ethics. That is another area in which theory may affect practice, as we shall see in the next chapter.

Medical ethics

12   How can moral philosophy help?

Some moral philosophy is usually included in courses on medical ethics given as part of the training of doctors and nurses. How can moral philosophy help? It is not a technique for solving practical problems but it can clarify the issues. For example, if the problem arises from a conflict of principles or claims, one may understand it more clearly in the light of philosophical theories which connect ethical principles in a coherent scheme. The main theories about the standard of morals are especially relevant. Debate about problems of medical ethics often invokes rights on the one hand (the right to life, the right to choose) and social consequences on the other. The different character of these two grounds of argument is brought out by relating them to the theories of intuitionism and utilitarianism.

I described intuitionism in Chapter 5 as a theory about self-evident principles of right action or duty. Some duties but not all (Kant called them duties of strict obligation) are correlated with a right held by the person to whom the duty is owed. The duty of A to pay a debt to B is correlated with a right of B against A that the debt be paid; the duty of all human beings not to kill others is correlated with a universal right not to be killed (a right to life). The second example needs a little elaboration since it often comes into discussions of medical ethics with the question whether the right to life implies a duty to take all possible measures to preserve life.

'Thou shalt not kill' is of course one of the Ten Commandments as given in the Authorized or King James Version of the Bible. (The Revised Version translates the original more accurately as 'Thou shalt do no murder'.) A nineteenth-century poet, Arthur Hugh Clough, wrote a satirical version of the Ten Commandments, 'The Latest Decalogue', in order to poke fun at a mere cloak of morality. It begins:

> Thou shalt have one God only; who
> Would be at the expense of two?

and it gives the sixth commandment as:

> Thou shalt not kill; but need'st not strive
> Officiously to keep alive.

Both are of course satirical. In the second quotation, Clough is deriding people who simply refrain from breaking basic rules and do not try to do some positive good. He is reminding us that conformity to prohibitions is not the whole of our moral duty. Some classical political theorists said, in the same spirit, that the 'natural right' to life goes beyond a right not to be killed and includes a right to be helped if one is in danger of starvation. Doctors need no reminding of their professional duty to preserve life, but modern medicine enables them to do so in circumstances where the value of that life is questionable. When such cases are discussed, Clough's couplet is often quoted to *support* refraining from 'heroic' measures that may properly be called officious striving. We are still left with the genuine question, how far does the right to life extend? Does it depend on the judgement of others about the worth of the life that can be maintained, or on the patient's known or presumed preference? If the former, it seems reasonable to weigh the worth or value of the quality of life against the cost of preserving it, the cost in terms of resources that could be used for other valuable ends or in terms of the burden imposed on the patient's family. But if, on the other hand, a judgement about the right to life depends on the preference of the patient, it does not seem appropriate to weigh that against 'costs', though it can be weighed against competing rights. The first way of looking at the situation is reminiscent of utilitarianism, the second of intuitionism.

Intuitionism is not completely opposed to utilitarianism. It agrees that we ought to promote as much happiness as possible, but it denies that this is the sole principle of right action. Utilitarian thinking obviously has to come into decisions about the allocation of resources, in health care as in other spheres of life. It must likewise come into policy for medical research, where the aim is to seek as much benefit as possible for mankind generally. But a different mode of thought usually governs the decisions of doctors and nurses about their duties to patients. It is still a matter of aiming at benefit, but the benefit is specifically for the patient, not for mankind at large; and if this duty to the patient comes into conflict with another duty, its moral force lies in its being a personal obligation to that patient. Utilitarianism misses out the vital personal element. A utilitarian will say that the rule which requires special attention for particular obligations, such as those of doctors to patients, has arisen because it is usually the best way to contribute to general happiness. He also says that since the principle of maximizing happiness underlies all moral rules, it affords the criterion for decision in cases of a conflict of duties.

Is that true? If it were, it should be especially apparent when the general principle of utility is patently one of the conflicting claims. That can happen when a medical-research programme requires withholding a promising treatment from critically ill patients until it has been tested to the hilt. As I said just now, utilitarian thinking comes into policy for medical research. When a new drug is tested, guidelines drawn from past experience require a very high success rate before the drug is approved for clinical use. I am told that the success rate in the experimental trials has to be something like 90 per cent. If it is less, efforts are of course made to improve it by modifying the drug. Suppose a research project of this kind has, in time, reached a success rate of 70 per cent; that is to say, there is a 70 per cent probability that a patient treated with the drug will benefit. The guidelines say this is still not good enough, although everyone will agree that it is highly promising. If withholding the treatment is obviously going to result in a number of deaths that could probably be prevented, is it perfectly clear that this is the right course?

A valuable discussion by Dr Michael Lockwood describes a fictional and some real-life examples.[1] Sinclair Lewis, in his novel *Martin Arrowsmith*, wrote of a medical researcher who believes he has discovered a viral agent that can prevent or cure certain diseases, including bubonic plague. An opportunity to make a decisive test arises when an island in the West Indies is struck by bubonic plague. The researcher, Arrowsmith, is sent out with strict instructions to divide the population into two groups and to inject one group only with the viral agent. When the results indicate a pretty high success rate, Arrowsmith wrestles with his conscience whether to stick to the rules or to inject all the inhabitants. If he sticks to the rules, a scientifically proven success could save thousands of lives in the future, as against a few hundred on the island, but of course he is deeply moved by the distress before his eyes. His resolve to keep to the rules is finally broken down when his wife catches the plague and dies.

Though Dr Lockwood does not say so, this example is less helpful than it might be. A utilitarian could well argue that a man who feels he is responsible for the death of his wife cannot make a fully rational comparison of the alternatives. It would be better to look at examples where the general utility of a research programme has to be weighed simply against the obligations of a doctor to his patients. Lockwood's account of examples in real life shows that some doctors accept the utilitarian line of argument but a much greater number do not. Further evidence of a consensus can be seen in a proposed code of ethics on

[1] 'Sins of omission? The non-treatment of controls in clinical trials', *Aristotelian Society Supplementary Volume* 57 (1983), pp. 307–22.

medical research accepted by the Council of Europe in 1990. Balancing 'the respect and dignity of the individual against the benefits of medical advances', the code declared: 'The fundamental principle is that the patient must always be seen as more important than any benefit to science or society.'[2] The need to enunciate the principle shows that not every-one thinks it obvious, but the outcome throws serious doubt on the utilitarian case.

Some utilitarians will say flatly that the majority opinion is misguided, but we can reasonably ask them how they know that. Others, less ready to fly in the face of general inclinations, will say that the greater weight attached to a doctor's personal obligation to his patients depends on its long-term utility, which can be greater than the obvious utility of the guidelines for research. But that strikes me as a fudge. We have no real evidence for thinking that the particular importance attached to special personal obligations is founded on their social utility. The doctor, the teacher, the parent or spouse, the friend, who feels a special obligation in that capacity, is not led to it by thoughts of social utility but rather by a sense of personal responsibility, a personal tie arising from the relation-ship. Any suggestion that these ideas have grown up as the actual, but unknown and unintended, effect of social utility is mere speculation, twisting facts to fit preconceived theory instead of finding a theory to fit the facts. We saw in Chapter 5 that utilitarianism fails to fit some cardinal facts about justice, and it seems to me that the same thing is true of health care.

The duties correlated with the right to life are plainly comprised in the second and first of the intuitionist principles listed on p. 44 above: refraining from harm to other people and promoting their happiness. The right to choose or decide for oneself is not obviously contained in those principles as I have set them out, but it is clearly implied in the overall Kantian principle of treating people as ends. I explained (p. 57) that this means helping them to fulfil their desires and allowing or enabling them to carry out their decisions. In discussions of medical ethics, the right to choose for oneself comes up very often under the name of 'autonomy', a technical term taken directly from Kant's theory of ethics. It is derived from a Greek word meaning self-rule. Autonomy is the ground for following a patient's preference when, for example, there is doubt whether to take exceptional measures to preserve life or whether to disclose the whole truth about his or her condition. Here again a utilitarian says that the value attached to autonomy rests on its general utility: deciding for oneself normally leads to more happiness than being

---

[2] Report in *The Times*, 20 Feb. 1990.

subject to 'paternalistic' decisions of the doctor. But do we know that this is true? A good many doctors say from their experience that disclosing the truth about a terminal illness has a devastating effect on the majority of patients even when they have asked for the truth. In any event, the point of respect for autonomy is not the general effect for most people but the right of a particular person in a particular situation. Utilitarianism obscures this, while Kantian theory makes it clearer.

Philosophy can also try to clarify issues in medical ethics by analysing a crucial concept. In discussions about abortion, experiments on embryos, the treatment of patients in a 'persistent vegetative state', or even the treatment of babies born with severe mental disabilities, some philosophers have fastened upon the concept of a person, taking the basic Kantian principle of ethics to be 'respect for persons' (or treating 'persons' as ends), and have defined a person in a way that rules out foetuses and the rest as persons. One such definition is that a person is a self-conscious being with long-term aims. This move does not put an immediate end to argument since others may say that the concept relevant for ethics includes the potentiality of being a person, but it does encourage us to ask what is the ground for common assumptions about the sanctity of human life. At the same time we should be wary of any suggestion that problems of genuine practical concern can be settled by definition. Anyone who finds a real moral problem in abortion or in the treatment of severely disabled infants has not been led to it by thoughts about 'persons'; and if a definition of 'person' rules out his concern, then either the definition or the reliance on the concept is misplaced. Drawing attention to the meaning of a key term or phrase can make a modest contribution to practical debate but it does no more than clear the air.

Another example is the distinction between acts and omissions, and especially between killing and letting die. There are situations in which it is very difficult, perhaps impossible, to apply the distinction firmly. If brain activity has ceased but heart and lungs can be kept going by a machine, is the act of switching off the machine an act of killing? And if the act of switching *on* the machine is a necessary condition for maintaining the heart and lung activity, is a deliberate omission to switch on the machine a causing of death, and if so, is it tantamount to an act of killing? To pose such questions and to bring out the complexity of the notion of causation is sometimes necessary; certainly the law has to face these questions and to use philosophical reasoning, as well as the advice of medical experts, in answering them. But here, too, philosophical discussion can frustrate the purpose of being helpful if it gives way to exaggeration. Doctors tend to be irritated when told that no clear distinction can be drawn between killing and letting die. Armchair theorists may dream up imaginary situations in which the distinction disappears, but in the actual practice of medicine, the doctors say, they know perfectly well whether a possible course of action would be killing or letting die. While there are difficult cases, they are exceptional and the doubt about them does not cast doubt on the vast majority of cases. It certainly is unhelpful to exaggerate the scope of the difficulty and say that there is no morally significant difference between acts and omissions. I once heard a philosopher put forward the following argument in a medical-ethics discussion of killing and letting die: if the government of our country were to donate £100,000 for the relief of famine in the Third World, that action would save the lives of 1,000 people who would otherwise starve to death; therefore the failure to make the donation is tantamount to killing those 1,000 people. You might just as well say that since my slipping a teaspoonful of poison into the coffee of my neighbour at dinner would kill him, my omission to do so is tantamount to rescuing him from an untimely death, for which he should be eternally grateful. In purely philosophical discussion, paradox can be useful in making us think about faulty logic, but when it is gratuitously thrown into a genuine practical concern it brings philosophy into disrepute.

Philosophy can be helpful in a more modest fashion by looking at concepts which keep on recurring in legal discussion of medical ethics. An example is 'the interests' or 'the best interests' of a person. The phrase recalls an idea familiar in utilitarian theory, but it is not at all clear that this is always what is intended.

The English Court of Appeal issued an important judgement in 1981[3] about a newly born baby suffering from Down's syndrome and from an intestinal blockage which would have been fatal within a few days if not removed. The parents decided to refuse consent to the operation because the child would in any event have the defects of Down's syndrome. The doctors, disagreeing with the view of the parents, contacted the local authority, which made the child a ward of court and applied for an order authorizing the operation. Their intention was that the future care of the child would, if necessary, be handed over to foster-parents, which is in fact what happened in the end. Both of the judges who constituted the Court of Appeal decided in favour of the local authority. Lord Justice Templeman said that the question to be determined was 'whether it is in the interests of this child to be allowed to die . . . or to have the operation', and he firmly chose the second alternative. He then went on to contemplate the possibility, in a hypothetical case, that the child's life would be so 'full of pain and suffering' (his colleague, Lord Justice

---

[3] *In re B (a Minor) (Wardship: Medical Treatment)*, [1981] 1 WLR 1421, CA.

Dunn, preferred to say 'intolerable') that the court might be driven to allowing her to die.

Now what can it mean to say that death is in the interests of someone? Since death will terminate his or her existence, how can one speak of there being any interest, positive or negative, arising from death? You can certainly say that in some circumstances the misery of a human life can vastly exceed its happiness, which is the line of thought followed by Lord Justice Templeman. You can also say that a human being, if capable of exercising choice, may prefer to die rather than to continue living in those circumstances, and that is what Lord Justice Dunn's 'intolerable' implies. It is still questionable whether either of these propositions entitles or morally requires anyone else to take action which would result in the death of the person concerned, but at least we have an intelligible account of the situation of that person.

The difficulty of using the term 'interests' in such a case came out in a later judgement of the Court of Appeal in 1990,[4] which also concerned a baby born with disabilities. The leading judgement was made by Lord Donaldson, Master of the Rolls. He noted that one of the barristers had quoted comments of two Court of Appeal judges in a 1982 case: both had said that it was impossible to compare the value of an injured child's life with a supposed value of non-existence. Lord Donaldson himself then quoted, with approval, a Canadian and an American judgement which said 'the court must decide what its ward would choose, if he were in a position to make a sound judgment.' The point of that statement was to rebut the idea that a parent or a court was entitled to judge that the quality of another person's life was 'so low as not to be deserving of continuance': the criterion should be the presumed choice of the person concerned. A baby cannot choose but we can consider the views of severely disabled people who are mature enough to judge whether their lives are worth living. Yet Lord Donaldson felt obliged to tie this view to the traditional idea of best interests: if the patient is a child who is not of an age to choose, the choice 'must be made solely *on behalf of the child* and in what the court or parents conscientiously believe to be his best interests'. He then reaffirmed the 1981 view of Lord Justices Templeman and Dunn. In order to decide what course of action is 'in the best interests of the child', there has to be a 'balancing exercise', taking account of 'the pain and suffering and quality of life which the child will experience if life is prolonged'. Lord Donaldson said that he preferred the formulation in the Canadian and American judgements but added

---

[4] *In re J (a Minor) (Wardship: Medical Treatment)*, [1991] Fam 33, CA. The judgement was delivered in October 1990 but appeared in the official Law Reports in 1991.

that it was 'probably merely another way of expressing the same concept' and he continued to speak of 'the best interests of the child'.

Another of the judges, Lord Justice Taylor, also quoted the comment that it is impossible to bring death into a comparison. Nevertheless, he said, if a prolonged life 'would be so cruel as to be intolerable', the court was 'entitled in the best interests of the child' to decide against artificial prolongation; 'the test must be whether the child in question, if capable of exercising sound judgment, would consider the life tolerable.'

Lord Donaldson was mistaken in suggesting that a person's 'choice' and his 'best interests' are two ways of expressing the same concept. A person's choice may be guided by the thought of his interests (though even then the two are not identical), but it need not. This is certainly true of the great majority of choices, which have nothing to do with the continuance of life, but let us confine ourselves to choices which are concerned with that. People who suffer terrible pain do not all take the same view about choosing or preferring an end to their lives, and the choice that they do make may be guided by their thought of the interests of their nearest and dearest as well as, or even instead of, thought about themselves. So, apart from the difference of meaning, choice can have a wider scope than the thought of one's own interests. Furthermore, the point of the Canadian judgement was to prefer the presumed choice of the person concerned to an external observer's estimate of 'what constitutes a liveable life'. This gives priority to the principle of autonomy over a paternalistic judgement of interests.

The confusing character of the term 'best interests' arose again in the distressing case of Tony Bland, which came before the courts in 1992–3.[5] This particular matter was far from being one of the crucial issues but it did cause difficulty for the judges. Tony Bland had been in a persistent vegetative state for over three years as the result of injuries received at a football ground disaster. His parents and doctors sought permission to discontinue treatment that sustained such life as was left to him. Sir Stephen Brown, the judge in the court of first instance, accepted the submission that it was 'in the best interests' of the patient to discontinue the treatment. The use of this phrase troubled several commentators, one of whom asked how could a patient who had lost all power of sensation be said to have any interests.

An answer to the question was given by Sir Thomas Bingham, Master of the Rolls, when the case came to the Court of Appeal. He said that pain and suffering must of course be ignored since the patient was insensate, but account could be taken of wider considerations. 'An

[5] *Airedale NHS Trust* v. *Bland*, [1993] 2 WLR 316, HL(E).

objective assessment of Mr. Bland's best interests, viewed through his eyes,' could give weight to the constant invasions of his body by the treatment, to his natural desire to be remembered as a cheerful teenager, to the ordeal imposed on his family, and even perhaps to the best use of finite resources. This statement suggests that 'best interests' in such circumstances should be interpreted as what the patient would probably choose or wish, and that this would take in the interests of other people as well as his own. Sir Thomas Bingham also implicitly recognized the difficulty of regarding death as an interest by saying instead that the prolongation of life in this situation was not a benefit.

The other two judges of the Court of Appeal agreed with the general tenor of Sir Thomas's view but they differed from each other about the relation of best interests to choice. Lord Justice Butler-Sloss thought that 'the American approach based on substituted judgment' (inferring what the patient would have chosen) had little in common with 'the objective best interests of the patient' as understood in English law; yet she agreed that Tony Bland's 'views, personality, how others including his family saw him', would form part of the assessment of his best interests. Lord Justice Hoffmann, on the other hand, emphasized the importance of choice, thought that best interests included respect paid to the probable views of the subject, and was ready 'to this extent' to subsume the American concept of 'substituted judgment . . . within the English concept of best interests'.

When the case came to the House of Lords, Lord Keith said the fundamental question was whether continuance of treatment 'would confer any benefit'. He felt some doubt about the form of the answer, 'his best interests favour discontinuance', because, with a permanently insensate being, 'it is difficult, if not impossible, to make any relevant comparison between continued existence and the absence of it'. Lord Goff agreed that 'it may be difficult to say that it is in his best interests that the treatment should be ended', and preferred to say 'his best interests no longer require' that the treatment should continue: where there is no benefit, there is 'no weighing operation to be performed'; the treatment 'is properly regarded as . . . useless' (later he used the word 'futile'). Like Lord Justice Butler-Sloss, he thought that the American 'substituted judgment test' was different from the concept of best interests.

As a result of all these reflections by judges, some difficulties have been acknowledged and avoided but there is still a lack of clarity in the phrase 'best interests'. It is a traditional concept in the law, and there are many situations in which it is appropriate: for example, when deciding who should have care of a child, or whether a person who is mentally incapable of consent should undergo an operation. In such circumstances it makes sense to think of a 'balancing exercise' of probable happiness and misery. But when the question is whether a patient should be allowed to die or should have a poor form of life artificially prolonged, the traditional idea of best interests does not really fit.

The most troublesome problems of medical ethics are subject to the rules of law and have to be settled for practical purposes in the courts. Judges see the clarification of key concepts as part of their own task, while appreciating that it has a philosophical character. For the general reader, philosophy can perhaps make a more useful contribution by reflecting on the wider context of medical ethics and the law, particularly in relation to traditional assumptions about the sanctity of human life. It is worth noting, incidentally, that in the Tony Bland case Lord Justice Hoffmann was most deeply exercised about the conflict between the sanctity of life and the right of self-determination (autonomy); he said that in his examination of the ethical issues he had been helped by conversation with two philosophers, and later in his judgement he quoted a third philosopher on the difficulty of deciding amid a conflict of basic principles.

Some problems of medical ethics are so baffling and yet so vital to society that they must be subject to legal decision. When the law deals with matters of ethics, it is intended to reflect the conscience of society. Social attitudes change over time, but only gradually in matters of ethics, and that too is reflected in the law. Scientific advance, in medicine as in other fields, is very rapid nowadays and that makes for changes in the outlook of medical practitioners, changes that may come upon them unawares. And so we find that in some areas of medical ethics a newly emerging attitude in medicine can conflict with a traditional attitude in the law. Since the conflict mirrors a conflict in society generally, it is not at all easy to say which should prevail.

Most of the difficulties, and certainly the most intractable difficulties, of medical ethics are moral dilemmas, situations in which a choice has to be made between conflicting moral claims. Moral dilemmas as such are not peculiar to medicine. Moral dilemmas are the very stuff of ethics in practice. Philosophers may worry their heads over doubts whether moral values are absolute or relative, objective or subjective, intrinsically disinterested or subservient to natural egoism; and sometimes people in real life are given pause by these questions. But the most common and the most genuine difficulties about ethics in practical life are those of choosing between conflicting claims. Apart from the moral dilemmas that are liable to face human beings in general, doctors have always had their own specific ethical problems, in consequence of which they have long had a code of professional ethics, reaching back at least to the time of Hippocrates in the 5th century BC. The primary purpose of the code was to inculcate an especially firm standard of moral conduct for a group whose specialized knowledge could serve devilish no less than angelic ends; but it also gave some guidance for dilemmas by insisting on the absolute character of two or three principles. Supposedly absolute principles, however, can themselves produce conflicts. The principle that a doctor must always try to preserve human life does not tell him what to do when he has to choose between the life of a mother in labour and the life of her child, or between the risk of a patient's death from an operation and the probability of a shortened life from his disease. That kind of dilemma is almost as old as medical science itself. It is not dilemmas as such that have turned medical ethics into front-page news.

The problems of medical ethics have come to the forefront of public attention in recent decades because the advance of medical science has opened up strikingly new possibilities for medical practice. In the past, the discovery of a new drug or the improvement of a surgical technique increased the capacity of doctors to cure or ward off disease, but the difference which this made was a difference of degree, hardly great enough to produce a new kind of moral dilemma. When the average span of life was sixty-five years, it seemed pure gain to be able to increase it to seventy. When a fair percentage of normal babies died at birth, it was pure gain for improved obstetrics to make such deaths exceptional. But there is a qualitative change in the ethical situation when medical advance can preserve life for people suffering from senile dementia or for newly born babies suffering from spina bifida or severe brain defects. It is not all pure gain now. A veterinary surgeon dealing with non-human animals would have no hesitation in 'putting down' old or newly born creatures that were so far removed from a state of normal good health. Our ethical tradition cherishes the principle that human life is sacred; but when it is reduced to a 'vegetative' state, should it still be held sacred?

It is the possibility of actual choice between life and death that gives rise to the most agonizing perplexity. There are other problems that have widespread serious consequences but are less critical in their immediate impact on moral choice. Some of the most striking advances in medical science pose problems about the allocation of resources, problems that are large in scale but not radically new in their ethical quality. For example, machines for kidney dialysis could save many lives if they were more widely available, but they are expensive. If enough money were provided to treat all who could benefit, there would have to be a saving elsewhere (in other parts of the health service or in some other field of government expenditure), or else the money would have to be raised by additional taxation. You and I may say that we are ready to pay higher taxes for this purpose; but then the same argument can be applied to lots of other social services, and there comes a point when the increase of taxes is counter-productive in its economic effects. Choices about the allocation of resources and the raising of revenue have to be made by the government of the day, not by individual doctors. Meanwhile, however, the doctors who do have dialysis units at their disposal are required to 'play God', to choose which patients shall have the treatment and which not. Even so, the dilemmas about the allocation and use of resources are not different in ethical character from those that have always faced governments and doctors. A section of the national community suffers from exceptionally severe unemployment or from the effects of storm or drought. A section of the international community suffers from famine or earthquake or simply from an undeveloped economy. To what extent should the government of this country allocate resources so as to help make special provision for these needs? In some of these examples, the problem of choice arises with the emergence of new needs as a result of natural events. It differs thereby from the problem of choice which arises as a result of the human invention of new but expensive machines to deal with old needs. Nevertheless, the ethical character of the choice is the same. That may not make it any easier to reach a decision, except to the extent that past practice on priorities may seem to afford a reasonable precedent. However, the familiarity of the type of problem deprives it of the agonizing element that tends to characterize a dilemma which is really new.

The dilemma of choosing between life and death can arise both in respect of the newly born and in respect of the terminally ill. Scientific advance has made it possible to preserve the lives of severely defective babies who in the past would necessarily have died, after a very short period, in the course of nature. The new possibility brought with it a genuinely new problem: should doctors follow the principle of preserving human life whenever they can, or should they refrain from using their new power in cases where the quality of life, extracted 'unnaturally', will be far below the normal? Scientific advance has also made it possible to prolong the lives of many people suffering from terminal illness. Here, too, the same sort of question can be asked: should doctors preserve human life whenever they can, or should they refrain from special efforts to 'go against nature' when the quality of the extra period of life for the patient is, by normal human standards, not worth living?

The dilemma is more acute in the first type of case than the second. The most important reason for this is that a terminally ill patient may be able and ready to declare his or her choice on the matter, and that should clearly count for more than the opinion of relatives or doctors. When the patient is a newly born baby, however, the choice has to be made by others, a choice which is all the more poignant because of the helplessness and the stultified potential of the baby. This brings me to a second reason why the dilemma is more acute in such a case than in dealing with terminal illness. Most of the people who are terminally ill have had a fair span of life; the little extra that exceptional measures can procure is like a drop in a pool. That does not remove the force of the obligation felt by a doctor to preserve human life whenever he can, or felt by a relative to retain the presence of a dear one. It does, however, put these feelings into perspective. I shall therefore now concentrate on the dilemma that can arise in the treatment of newly born babies with severe defects.

Issues of life and death have traditionally come within the purview of the law. Whatever may be thought of the plethora of rights claimed in recent times to be fundamental human rights, the right to life is undoubtedly basic, calling for the protection of the law. All systems of law, so far as I am aware, have given priority to the protection of human life in treating the prohibition of murder as a fundamental law. But it would be far from true to say that all systems of law have protected the life of the handicapped child, or indeed any child, against the interests or supposed interests of parents or society generally. Ancient Sparta is notorious for its custom of exposing weak infants on the mountainside. The practice was not unknown in other parts of the ancient Greek world. Under the law of the Roman Republic the father of a family had the right of life and death over his children, as over his slaves, and sometimes used it; and although this power fell into disuse in the period of the Empire, it survived for the exposure of weak infants until AD 374, half-a-century after the Roman Empire became Christian. Infanticide of one kind and another, and especially in the case of malformed babies, has been and still is practised in many, though by no means all, non-western societies. Do these facts require that we in modern western societies should steel ourselves to be 'sensible' or 'realistic' and to shake off, so far as handicapped infants are concerned, the inhibitions which we have inherited from religious or humanistic doctrine about the natural right to life?

A boldly affirmative answer to this question is given by Dr Helga Kuhse and Professor Peter Singer in their book, *Should the Baby Live? The Problem of Handicapped Infants* (1985). It is a comprehensive and searching examination of its subject, and part of its practical proposals would command wide support. But whereas most other practical proposals for a relaxation of the law have deliberately been confined to allowing a severely handicapped baby to die, Kuhse and Singer go further in recommending that painless killing of the baby should be lawful. Like a number of other philosophers, they have persuaded themselves that there is no valid distinction between killing and letting die, and since they are utilitarians they regard a painless killing as preferable to a drawn-out and distressing process of natural death. However, they add to this argument another one designed to show that the belief in the sanctity of human life is a 'deviant tradition', dependent upon the peculiar religious doctrines of Judaism and Christianity, and less reasonable than the widespread practice of infanticide found among many tribal societies and in some other cultures which were undoubtedly civilized, such as ancient Greece and eighteenth-century Japan. They explain the peculiarity of the Judaeo-Christian tradition as follows. Ancient Judaism abhorred infanticide because its religious doctrine emphasized fertility ('Be fruitful and multiply'). Christianity added to this the doctrine that human life belongs to God, who alone has the right to dispose of it, and the doctrine of original sin, in consequence of which an unbaptized infant that died was doomed to eternal hell.

This supposed explanation of the moral disapproval of infanticide is used as an argument against the traditional assumption of the sanctity of human life. It serves as a critical evaluation of that assumption. Is it sound?

A scientific explanation of a pattern of behaviour is incomplete if it carries us no further than religious belief. Explanation, or rather justification, in terms of religious doctrine can satisfy one who believes in the doctrine, since for him the word of God is the ultimate ground for acceptance. But for religious sceptics like Kuhse and Singer, the causal power of religious doctrine stands itself in need of causal explanation, to be sought in empirical data such as psychological, social, or economic conditions. Thus the alleged peculiarity of Judaeo-Christian disapproval of infanticide is not adequately explained by the alleged peculiarity of a religious command to procreate or by the religious doctrine that human life belongs to God. We need to be told, in empirical terms of explanation, why those religious doctrines were adopted. In fact an emphasis on fertility is not peculiar to the religion of ancient Judaism; it was the norm among ancient peoples until the dangers of over-population became apparent. The Christian doctrine that human life belongs to God is an expression, rather than an explanation, of the moral belief that it is wrong to take human life, including one's own life. As for the doctrine that an unbaptized infant who dies is condemned to eternal hell, the practical implication of this is not that no infant should be killed or left to die, but that no infant should be left unbaptized before it dies.

However, it is more to the point to observe that the moral disapproval of infanticide is not peculiar to Judaism and Christianity. As I mentioned earlier, the practice, although common, is not universal among primitive peoples; it was rare among the American Indians, for example, and in much of Africa. Kuhse and Singer themselves note that 'even before the rise of Christianity some philosophical and religious schools, other than Judaism, expressed a strong respect for human life', though they fairly add that 'such views were only held by a minority'.[6] The views even of a minority require explanation, and the explanation in this case cannot lie in the religious doctrines of Judaism and Christianity. It makes more sense to look for a common explanation, in empirical terms, of both the biblical and the non-biblical ethics of a respect for human life.

Adam Smith was not one of the world's greatest moral philosophers but he displayed, in life as in theory, an exceptional degree of moral sensitivity, despite the hard-headed realism of his masterly grasp of economics and sociology. Two things impressed him especially as morally repulsive, slavery and the ancient practice of exposing weak infants. He knew that slavery was and long had been widely pervasive; he doubted whether it would ever be eradicated. He also knew that the exposure of infants had been practised in many of the Greek states besides Sparta and likewise in Rome, and that it continued among 'all savage nations' in his own day. This realistic appraisal of sociological fact led him to explain and excuse the practice in 'that rudest and lowest state of society', often subjected to 'extreme indigence'. But it did not lead him to mitigate his condemnation of the practice 'in the latter ages of Greece', where it 'was permitted from views of remote interest or conveniency'.[7] Smith's reaction did not depend on biblical doctrine but on sympathetic feeling. Is it not likely that the biblical doctrine too, and the similar (minority) views which arose in the ancient world outside the biblical tradition, should be explained as the effect of natural human feelings, overridden in many societies by ideas of economic necessity? The advances of medical science in the twentieth century have presented us with a new or a sharper problem; but we have no more reason than Adam Smith in the eighteenth century to suppose that we should learn our ethics from practices, however widespread, that strike us as immoral.

In describing Adam Smith's reaction, I coupled the exposure of weak infants with the practice of slavery. The analogy between the two is worth pursuing. Kuhse and Singer also refer to the analogy of slavery in acknowledging that the prevalence of a practice does not make it morally right. There is, however, more to the analogy than prevalence. Slavery

[6] p. 114.
[7] *The Theory of Moral Sentiments*, V. 2. 15.

has taken many forms, but the one essential feature that is common to all of them is the notion of treating a human being as the property of another human being, to be used and disposed of as that other may wish. The same feature characterizes the historically common forms of infanticide and also some of the thinking that goes on today about the problem of handicapped infants.

In arguments about handicapped infants one consideration is the practical possibility for the parents of trying again and having a normal baby. It is entirely proper to give weight to this, but is it proper to assume that the parents are therefore entitled to 'scrap' the existing baby, as if they were disposing of an uncomfortable and unwanted chair in order to make room for another? The begetting of a child is commonly taken to imply responsibilities for the parents. If the child turns out to be so handicapped that the responsibility of caring for him or her will be exceptionally burdensome and virtually unending, the parents can reasonably claim to decline that responsibility; but it is not for them to say that the child should therefore have no one to take over the responsibility. A child 'belongs' to his parents, biological or adoptive, in the sense that they rather than anyone else have the right and the duty to nurture him, on the understanding that they will accept the duty. If they do not accept the duty, they lose the right to exclude others from the position of caring for the child and determining his future. Children are not the property of parents. If I own a material object, perhaps one that is beautiful or rare, I am entitled to destroy it or to mar it by neglect or ill-use, however much other people may deplore my behaviour. This is not the position of parents in relation to their children. The religious doctrine that human life belongs to God may be questionable for its ban on suicide but not for its more general implication that no human life belongs to, is at the disposal of, another human being.

In the first edition of this book I said that moral philosophy, as I see it, has three main branches. First, there are logical problems about moral concepts and judgements. In the early stages of the subject, these were regarded as ontological problems; that is to say, problems about the kind of being or status which should be attributed to values: are they 'objective' or 'absolute'; or, alternatively, are they 'subjective' or 'relative' (to the particular feelings of an individual person or of most people in his society)? Nowadays we can see that more progress is made by looking at the problems in terms of logic and the use of language. Secondly, there are criteriological problems, questions about the criteria or standards of moral judgement, whether in private life or in the wider context of social and political organization. What makes a right action right? What makes a good thing good? What makes an unjust situation unjust, and what would help to make it more just? Can the criteria or standards be tied up in a coherent, and preferably a simple, scheme? Thirdly, there are problems about the relation of moral thinking to other bodies of thought. Do the presuppositions of ethics conflict with the presuppositions of natural science, or of theology? Can the idealism of ethics fit in with the tough-mindedness that seems necessary in practical politics or economics?

In all these areas of discussion there is obviously much more to be said. Recent moral philosophy has become highly sophisticated about the logical problems, but I did not dwell on them for too long because I think that most beginners see more easily the point of the criteriological problems. In the third area of discussion, the most intriguing and most intractable problem is that of free will and determinism, which I therefore singled out for illustration. But even that problem alone has far wider ramifications than appear in my account.

In the second edition I have added two further topics. Ethics and evolution is another illustration of the relations between moral thinking and natural science. The topic has suffered from a good deal of confused thought, but it retains a strong interest for scientists and Professor James Rachels's recent book shows why it should receive more attention from philosophers. The second topic, medical ethics, does not fit neatly into my classification of three branches of moral philosophy. Although it concerns the relation of ethics to medicine and the law, its problems are practical rather than theoretical. Still, philosophical discussion can help a little with conceptual aspects of the practical problems, and moral philosophers have given much attention to them in recent years. I think that both topics should be of interest to the general reader. Like the earlier topics, they illustrate the value of philosophical thinking in pursuing clarity and critical argument.

As I have said in the preface, the book is intended to be an introduction. It has aimed at giving helpful first words, and occasionally some second words, but nothing like the last word, on the subjects with which it deals. Although I have tried to present fairly arguments for opposed theories on all the major topics, I have not hesitated to disclose my own views. If I have succeeded at all in conveying the critical outlook which is essential to philosophy, the reader will understand that the proper response to my conclusions is not just to accept them without further thought but to continue the argument.

Suggestions for further reading

Classical texts

Plato: *Republic*. Of the many English translations I prefer the one by F.M. Cornford (Oxford University Press, 1941; paperback edition, 1969). The translation by H.D.P. Lee (Penguin Books, paperback, 1955) also represents well the spirit of the original Greek.

Aristotle: *Nicomachean Ethics*. There are modern English translations by Sir (W.) David Ross (Oxford University Press, 1925; paperback, 1980) and by J.A.K. Thomson (Allen & Unwin, 1953; Penguin Books, paperback, revised by Hugh Tredennick and Jonathan Barnes, 1976).

Thomas Hobbes: *Human Nature* (otherwise known as *The Elements of Law*, Part I); *Leviathan*, Part 1; *Of Liberty and Necessity*. *Human Nature* and *Of Liberty and Necessity* are included in a paperback volume, Thomas Hobbes: *Body, Man, and Citizen*, ed. R.S. Peters (Collier Books, New York, 1962). *Leviathan* is available in various paperback editions (Collier–Macmillan, 1963; Penguin Books, 1968; Dent, Everyman Library, 1973).

Benedict de Spinoza: *Ethics*, Parts III and IV. The most suitable English translation is by W. Hale White, revised by Amelia H. Stirling (Duckworth, corrected 3rd edn., 1898; Oxford University Press, 4th edn., 1910).

Joseph Butler: *Fifteen Sermons preached at the Rolls Chapel*; *Dissertation of the Nature of Virtue*. There is a convenient modern edition by T.A. Roberts (Society for Promoting Christian Knowledge, paperback, 1970).

David Hume: *Treatise of Human Nature*, Book III; *Enquiry concerning the Principles of Morals*. The most suitable editions of both works are those edited by L.A. Selby-Bigge, revised by P.H. Nidditch (Clarendon Press, hardback and paperback: *Treatise*, 1978; *Enquiries concerning Human Understanding and concerning the Principles of Morals*, 1975). There are also paperback editions of the *Treatise* published by Penguin Books (1969) and by Fontana/Collins (Books II-III, 1972).

Richard Price: *Review of the Principal Questions in Morals*. There is a modern edition by D.D. Raphael (Clarendon Press, corrected reprint, 1974).

Adam Smith: *The Theory of Moral Sentiments*. There is a modern edition by D.D. Raphael and A.L. Macfie (Clarendon Press, corrected reprint, 1991; paperback reprint, Liberty Classics, 1982).

Immanuel Kant: *Groundwork of the Metaphysic of Morals*. The best English translation is by H.J. Paton. It translates the German title as *Groundwork ...* but carries the main title, *The Moral Law* (Hutchinson, 1948; paperback, 1956).

Jeremy Bentham: *Introduction to the Principles of Morals and Legislation.* There is a modern edition by J.H. Burns and H.L.A. Hart (Athlone Press, 1970; paperback reprint, Methuen, 1982).

John Stuart Mill: *Utilitarianism; On Liberty.* Both essays are included in a volume of the Everyman Library (Dent, new edition, hardback and paperback, 1972) and in a Fontana paperback (Collins, 1962).

Henry Sidgwick: *The Methods of Ethics* (Macmillan, revised and corrected 7th edn., 1907; reprint, hardback and paperback, Hackett, 1981).

Relevant extracts from Hobbes, Butler, Hume, Price, Smith, and Bentham may be found in D.D. Raphael (ed.), *British Moralists 1650–1800* (Clarendon Press, hardback and paperback, 1969; reprint, hardback and paperback, Hackett, 1991).

A selection of twentieth-century works

G.E. Moore: *Principia Ethica* (Cambridge University Press, 1903; paperback, 1959); *Ethics* (Home University Library, 1912; Oxford University Press, paperback, 1966).

Sir (W.) David Ross: *The Right and the Good* (Clarendon Press, 1930; reprint, hardback and paperback, Hackett, 1988); *Foundations of Ethics* (Clarendon Press, 1939).

Charles L. Stevenson: *Ethics and Language* (Yale University Press, 1944).

H.A. Prichard: *Moral Obligation* (Clarendon Press, 1949).

R.M. Hare: *The Language of Morals* (Clarendon Press, 1952; paperback, 1964); *Freedom and Reason* (Clarendon Press, 1963; paperback, 1965); *Moral Thinking* (Clarendon Press, hardback and paperback, 1981).

P.H. Nowell-Smith: *Ethics* (Penguin Books, paperback, 1954; Blackwell, hardback, 1957).

Kurt Baier: *The Moral Point of View* (Cornell University Press, 1958; Random House, abridged paperback, 1965).

Richard B. Brandt: *Ethical Theory* (Prentice-Hall, 1959); *A Theory of the Good and the Right* (Clarendon Press, 1979).

Philippa Foot (ed.): *Theories of Ethics* (Oxford University Press, paperback, 1967).

R.S. Downie and Elizabeth Telfer: *Respect for Persons* (Allen & Unwin, hardback and paperback, 1969).

G.J. Warnock: *The Object of Morality* (Methuen, hardback and paperback, 1971).

John Rawls: *A Theory of Justice* (Harvard University Press, 1971; Clarendon Press, 1972; Oxford University Press, paperback, 1973).

Bernard Williams: *Morality* (Harper & Row, 1972; Penguin Books, paperback, 1973).

J.J.C. Smart and Bernard Williams: *Utilitarianism, for and against* (Cambridge University Press, hardback and paperback, 1973).

J.L. Mackie: *Ethics* (Penguin Books, paperback, 1977).

Alan Gewirth, *Reason and Morality* (Chicago University Press, 1978).

Alasdair MacIntyre, *After Virtue* (Duckworth, 1981; enlarged 2nd edition, hardback and paperback, 1985).

James Rachels, *Created from Animals: The Moral Implications of Darwinism* (Oxford University Press, 1990).

Index